Twelve Essential Upanishads

Volume I

Brihad Aranyaka Upanishad

The Forest Teachings

Twelve Essential Upanishads

Three Volume Series
English translation with annotations
Shukavak N. Dasa

ISBN 978-1-889756-00-4

Volume I
Brihad Aranyaka Upanishad:
The Forest Teachings

Volume II
Chandogya Upanishad:
Teachings from the High Chant

Volume III
Taitiriya, Aitareya, Kaushitaki,
Kena, Katha, Isha, Shvetashvatara,
Mundaka, Prashna, & Mandukya
Upanishads

ISBN 978-1-889756-33-2

ISBN 978-1-889756-04-2

Twelve Essential Upanishads

Volume I

Brihad Aranyaka Upanishad

The Forest Teachings

Translation and Annotations

Shukavak N. Dasa

श्री

SRI PUBLICATIONS

SANSKRIT RELIGIONS INSTITUTE

LOS ANGELES

SRI PUBLICATIONS
SANSKRIT RELIGIONS INSTITUTE
WWW.SANSKRIT.ORG
SAN 299-2892

Twelve Essential Upanishads Volume I
Brihad Aranyaka Upanishad: The Forest Teachings
LCCN 2023934545
ISBN 978-1-889756-03-5 (Hardcover)
ISBN 978-1-889756-00-4 (Paperback)
ISBN 978-1-889756-02-8 (EPUB)

Cover photo: A Hindu priest in Kerala, India performs a fire sacrifice (*agni-hotra*) and throws offerings into the consecrated fire.

Acknowledgements

I thank Dr. Vijay Arora, Ash and Nita Patel, Archana and Akhil Sheth, and Vikas Sharma and family for their generous support publishing these volumes. I also thank Robert Arconti for editing and proofreading, along with Sukulina Dasi for layout, book design, and indexing.

About the Author

Shukavak N. Dasa holds a Ph.D. in South Asian Studies and a Master's degree in Sanskrit grammar from the University of Toronto. He regularly lectures on Hinduism and has played a key role in the development of Hindu temples across the United States and Canada.

He has officiated thousands of Hindu weddings and performed a wide range of rituals in North America, Europe, and India. With deep knowledge of Sanskrit and the symbolic meaning behind Hindu rites, Shukavak is known for making complex traditions accessible and enlightening for diverse audiences—including both lifelong practitioners and those new to the faith.

This translation was undertaken by a Westerner who is also a dedicated practitioner of Hinduism. With a nuanced understanding of the distinction between faith and belief, and drawing from his Western education and personal spiritual practice, the author approaches these sacred texts with both reverence and a desire to find meaning relevant to a Western context. His unique perspective bridges two worlds: rooted in Western thought, yet deeply engaged with Indian spiritual traditions.

www.Shukavak.com

A Note on Transliteration and Italicization

The English alphabet has twenty-six basic written sounds. The Sanskrit alphabet has forty-six basic written sounds. That's twenty additional sounds that English does not have, which are expressed by twenty different letters. So when we try to match the sounds of one alphabet to another, if there are not enough letters to make this match, we employ a system of diacritical marks to extend the range of the smaller alphabet. For example, English has just one "a" sound. Sanskrit has three "a" sounds. So to extend the letter "a," we add two separate diacritical marks. In this way we get "a" plus two additional "a" sounds, "ā" and "ā3." Similarly, English has one sibilant, "s," whereas Sanskrit has three sibilants. In this way we get "s" plus "ṣ" and "ś". Additionally, Sanskrit has four nasal sounds while English has only one. In this way we get "n" plus "ñ," "ṅ" and "ṇ." And there are more sounds that employ diacritics, and naturally each diacritical notation has a slightly different pronunciation.

A good example of how this actually works is with the word Krishna. Properly expressed using diacritical notation, this word should be written as Kṛṣṇa. The anglicization "Krishna" is just an approximation of the sound expressed by the diacritical notation Kṛṣṇa. But who can understand the sounds created with diacritical marks without proper training? It is a difficult matter.

In this publication, in order to simplify the words for the non-technical reader, we have elected to not use diacritical notation in the case of book titles and proper names. Consequently, Ṛg Veda has become Rig Veda, the name Gārgī has become Gargi, Īśopaniṣad becomes Isha Upanishad, etc. The one notable exception is with the words *brahma* and Brahmā. When this distinction comes up, it is explained in the annotation. Following this standard we have hopefully made it easier for the non-technical reader to at least pronounce proper names and titles. Otherwise, the standard use of diacritical marks has been employed for all words that are not proper names or book titles.

As far as italicization is concerned, generally book titles are italicized. In this publication, however, in order to streamline the text, which already has so many italicized Sanskrit words, I have elected not to italicize the titles of books.

Abbreviations

AU Aitareya Upanishad
BG Bhagavad Gita
BU Brihad Aranyaka Upanishad
ChU Chandogya Upanishad
IU Isha Upaniṣad
KauU Kaushitaki Upanishad
KeU Kena Upanishad
KU Katha Upanishad
MB Mahabharata
MaiU Maitri Upanishad
ManU Mandukya Upanishad
MS Manu Samhita
MuU Mundaka Upanishad
PU Prashna Upanishad
R Ramayana
RV Rig Veda
SK Sankhya Karika
SU Shvetashvatara Upanishad
TA Taitiriya Aranyaka
TU Taitiriya Upanishad
VS Vasishtha Smriti

Table of Contents

Abbreviations ix
Introduction to the Upanishads xv
Introduction to Brihad Aranyaka Upanishad 1

First *Adhyāya*

First *Brāhmaṇa* 4
The World as a Sacrificial Horse
Second *Brāhmaṇa* 6
Creation
Third *Brāhmaṇa* 10
The High Chant
The Creation of Evil in the World
and the Superiority of Breath
Fourth *Brāhmaṇa* 20
The Creation
Fifth *Brāhmaṇa* 30
Seven Kinds of Food
The Lord of Creatures as the Year 35
The Three Worlds 36
The Rite of Transference 36
The Competition of the Senses 38
Sixth *Brāhmaṇa* 40
The World as Name, Form and Action

Second *Adhyāya*

First *Brāhmaṇa* 42

Talks Between a Priest and a King

Second *Brāhmaṇa* 49

The Metaphor of the Body

Third *Brāhmaṇa* 52

Two Forms of *Brahma*

Fourth *Brāhmaṇa* 56

The Joy of Soul

Conversation between a Husband and a Wife

Fifth *Brāhmaṇa* 60

The Honey Teachings

Sixth *Brāhmaṇa* 65

The Lineage of Teachers and Students

Third *Adhyāya*

First *Brāhmaṇa* 68

The King's Challenge

Conversations with Yajnavalkya

Second *Brāhmaṇa* 74

The Senses and Their Objects

Third *Brāhmaṇa* 78

Where Performers of the Horse Sacrifice Go

Fourth *Brāhmaṇa* 79

The *Ātmā* within All

Fifth *Brāhmaṇa* 81

The *Ātmā* within All

Sixth *Brāhmaṇa* 82

Gargi Questions Yajnavalkya

The Support of the Worlds

Seventh *Brāhmaṇa* 85

Uddalaka Questions Yajnavalkya

The Force Within

Eighth *Brāhmaṇa* 91

Gargi Questions Yajnavalkya Once More

Ninth *Brāhmaṇa* 95

The Number of Gods

Fourth *Adhyāya*

First *Brāhmaṇa* 112

Talks Between Janaka and Yajnavalkya

What is *Brahma*?

Second *Brāhmaṇa* 120

Talks between Janaka and Yajnavalkya Continued

The Destination of the Soul

Third *Brāhmaṇa* 122

Talks Between Janaka and Yajnavalkya Continued

The Light of Man

Fourth *Brāhmaṇa* 135

Talks Between Janaka and Yajnavalkya Continued

The Process of Dying

Fifth *Brāhmaṇa* 144

Talks between Yajnavalkya and Maitreyi

Sixth *Brāhmaṇa* 149

The Lineage of Teachers and Students

Fifth *Adhyāya*

First *Brāhmaṇa* 152

Fullness and The Implicate Order

Second *Brāhmaṇa* 153

Da Da Da!

Third *Brāhmaṇa* 156

The Heart

Fourth *Brāhmaṇa* 156

The Real

Fifth *Brāhmaṇa* 156

Creation

Sixth *Brāhmaṇa* 159

The Lord in the Heart

Seventh *Brāhmaṇa* 159

Brahma as lightning

Eighth *Brāhmaṇa* 160

Speech and the Milk Cow

Ninth *Brāhmaṇa* 160

The Universal Fire Within

Tenth *Brāhmaṇa* 160

Leaving this world

Eleventh *Brāhmaṇa* 161

The Sadness of Mortal Life

Twelfth *Brāhmaṇa* 162

Food and Life Force

Thirteenth *Brāhmaṇa* 163

Uktha, Yajus, Sāman, Kṣatra as Life Force

Fourteenth *Brāhmaṇa* 164

Gāyatrī

Fifteenth *Brāhmaṇa* 170
Prayer of the Dying

Sixth *Adhyāya*
First *Brāhmaṇa* 172
Breath: The Oldest and the Greatest
Second *Brāhmaṇa* 176
Life after Death
Third *Brāhmaṇa* 184
A Fire Ritual for Greatness
Fourth *Brāhmaṇa* 190
Procreation and Sacrifice
Fifth *Brāhmaṇa* 200
The Lineage of Teachers and Students in the Vajaseneyi School

Sanskrit Glossary 206
Index 216

Introduction to the Upanishads

Reading an ancient document is like looking through the lens of a powerful telescope. The light that reaches the telescope has traveled huge distances before it finally reaches the lens of the telescope and eye of the observer. This light may be thousands of light years old, and so the observer is looking at the way things were at the time the light first began its journey. One is truly looking back in time! Similarly, the text of an ancient document is a snapshot of how things were at the time the particular document was composed. These Upanishads are ancient religious documents first composed thousands of years ago, and therefore, as we read them, we are looking back in time, seeing the state of religious thinking and practice in India at that time. The word *upaniṣad* refers to an esoteric or secret doctrine and so these Upanishads are a collection of ancient mystical teachings from a very ancient time.

The religious writings of Hinduism are collectively grouped under what is called the Vedas. The word *veda* just means "knowledge." The word is derived from the Sanskrit root *vid,* meaning "to know." So the Vedas are literally the knowing of ancient India. Today these Vedas are in two parts, the Shruti Vedas and the Smriti Vedas. We might call these two divisions the "really, really old," and the "just old." The Shruti Vedas are described as *a-pauruṣeya,* whereas the Smriti Vedas are described as *pauruṣeya*. The word *pauruṣeya* means "man-made" and *a-pauruṣeya* means "not man-made." Man-made means writings that were composed and written by a human being. These include such writings as the Mahabharata, the Ramayana, and the many Puranas. Various human writers, such as Vyasa, Valmiki and Badarayana, are the traditional authors credited with composing and recording these Smriti Vedas. The Shruti Vedas, on the other hand, have no such human authors. They are described as works that were "heard" in the hearts of semi-divine beings known as *ṛṣis*. Generally, the Shruti Vedas command higher authority than the Smriti Vedas, even though most of modern Hinduism follows the Smriti Vedas. Consequently, the stories of Rama and Sita, including the life of Hanuman, and the words of Krishna in the Bhagavad Gita are all part of the Smriti Vedas. So too are the stories of Shiva, Parvati, Ganesha and Durga.

The Upanishads fall within the purview of the Shruti Vedas and therefore hold the highest authority. The foundations of the Shruti Vedas are the four Vedas: Rig, Yajur, Sama and Atharva. Each of these four Vedas are divided into four branches called *śakhas*: the *chandas*, the *brāhmaṇas*, the *araṇyakas*, and the *upaniṣads*. Therefore, each Upanishad is connected to one of these four Vedas. Thus, some Upanishads are connected to the Rig Veda while others are connected to the Yajur Veda, the Sama Veda or the Atharva Veda.

In general, over a hundred Upanishads are known, of which just over a dozen or so are considered the oldest and most important.

These are called the principal (*mukhya*) Upanishads. Many Upanishads are later and some are even considered apocryphal. These later Upanishads, numbering about ninety-five, are often referred to as minor Upanishads and are dated from the first millennium CE right up until the fourteenth century CE. Commentators such as Shankara and Madhva have written commentaries on just ten of the principal Upanishads, but it is common to see publications of eleven, thirteen and eighteen Upanishads. The present publication presents twelve such principal Upanishads.

These principal Upanishads were traditionally memorized and passed down orally and are considered to predate the Common Era. Unfortunately, there is no scholarly consensus on their actual date or even which ones are pre- or post-Buddhist. The Brihad Aranyaka is seen as particularly ancient by current scholarship and therefore considered the oldest.

Patrick Olivelle, a Sanskrit philologist and Indologist, gives the following chronology for these principal Upanishads:

> The Brihad Aranyaka and the Chandogya are the two earliest Upanishads. They are edited texts, some of whose sources are much older than others. The two texts are pre-Buddhist; they may be placed in the seventh to sixth centuries BCE, give or take a century or so.
>
> The three other early prose Upanishads—Taittiriya, Aitareya, and Kausitaki— come next; all are probably pre-Buddhist and can be assigned

> to the sixth to fifth centuries BCE.
>
> The Kena is the oldest of the verse Upanishads, followed by the Katha, Isha, Shvetasvatara and Mundaka. All these Upanishads were composed probably in the last few centuries BCE.
>
> The two late prose Upanishads, the Prashna and the Mandukya, cannot be much older than the beginning of the common era.

These older principal Upanishads have naturally inspired a vast commentary tradition, the most important of which are the commentaries of Shankara Acharya, whose date is generally accepted around 700 CE. Shankara wrote many works during his lifetime, perhaps the most important of which are his commentaries on ten of the principal Upanishads, his Bhagavad Gita commentary and his Brahma Sutra commentary. These are the so-called *prasthāna-trayi,* or three foundational works that form the basis of *vedānta* theology.

Vedānta was an attempt to forge a synthesis and thereby find a "final conclusion" (*siddhānta*) to the Vedas, including both the Shruti Vedas and the Smriti Vedas. It was an early attempt to unify and smooth out the contradictions within the Vedas. Shankara's version of this Vedanta is known as *advaita*, but other commentators, such as Ramanuja (circa 1050 CE) and Madhva (circa 1200 CE), have their own schools of *vedānta*, also based on the *prasthāna-trayi,* known respectively as *vaśiṣṭhādvaita* and *dvaita*. Shankara's Advaita Vedanta by far holds the greatest popularity. Many followers of *vedānta* think that *vedānta* means Advaita Vedanta. They may not know there are competing forms of *vedānta*, that Madhva's Dvaita Vedanta is diametrically opposed to Shankara's Advaita Vedanta or that both synthesize a form of *vedānta* out of the very same *prasthāna-trayi* used by Shankara. They may not realize, for example, that the famous dictum *tat tvam asi* (that you are), which Shankara so commonly quotes, can also be legitimately read as *a-tat tvam asi* (that you are not), as Madhva reads this dictum.

Unfortunately, the intense impact of Shankara and the subsequent commentators following in his line of Advaita Vedanta have so dominated the tradition as to blot out these other expressions of *vedānta*. In many ways the tradition has, in effect, been frozen to the middle of the eighth century CE, yet we forget that these Upanishads belong to an age at least a thousand years before Shankara and even more prior to the times of Ramanuja and Madhva. So even Shankara Acharya comes quite late given the age of these Upanishads, yet such total dominance by Shankara and his followers has led to a stifling of newer and more modern forms of understanding and interpretation. Upanishadic scholarship tends to be stuck on the *vedānta* of eighth century India.

But from a modern perspective, we can legitimately ask why must there even be a *vedānta* in the first place? Why try to solve the inherent contradictions that exist within the Upanishads and the Bhagavad Gita or between the Shruti Vedas and the Smriti

Vedas? Why try to smooth out the tradition? The time differences between the two divisions of the Vedas alone are immense. Of course there are going to be differences and contradictions. Even the time differences between the various principal Upanishads span centuries. Of course there are going to be contradictions. Why must a religious tradition be perfectly uniform and consistent? Is it a matter of religious faith that drives this need to synthesize and smooth out a religious tradition—that if contradictions are found, they pose a challenge to religious faith and so must be resolved?

Perhaps modern comparative religion can help us resolve this problem and move on from eighth century India. One of the great accomplishments of modern comparative religion is the distinction that can be made between belief and faith. This was first brought to our attention by the theologian Wilford Cantwell Smith, who made this distinction back in the 1960s, in his book *The Meaning and End of Religion.* There he drew the distinction that within what we call religion are actually two components, an accumulated religious tradition and religious faith itself. The architecture, music, scriptures, doctrines, forms of dress, prayers, and even foods, etc., all form what he called the accumulated religious tradition. And then lying at the foundation of this accumulated tradition is the actual religious faith itself. The two interact: Faith produces the religious tradition in the first place and then in turn is nurtured and supported by that accumulated tradition.

If we accept this distinction, that belief and faith are not the same, then we realize that what one believes, the doctrines, the creeds, the theology, etc., are part of an accumulated tradition and therefore subject to change. Even the various forms of *vedānta* are part of this accumulated tradition. Of course beliefs will change over time as our understanding of the world changes. And yet a strong religious tradition is informed by its basic religious faith, which tends not to change. If we fail to see this distinction and think that religious faith and religious belief are the same, we force ourselves to become reactive and push ourselves into extreme positions of having to justify that faith when beliefs are challenged by changing circumstances. This often pushes us into anti-intellectual positions. A challenge to one's beliefs can easily create a crisis of faith; but when one understands the difference between belief and religious faith, then beliefs can change without affecting one's religious faith.

For a religious practitioner this is a liberating idea. One becomes freed from the need to rationalize or dismiss new circumstances. In the Western world probably the best example is Darwin's theory of evolution and how that was attacked when *Origin of Species* first appeared in 1859. Darwin was a direct challenge to the Christian beliefs of the day and therefore a challenge to Christian faith. Even today the attacks and denials still continue, particularly from Christian fundamentalism, which generally still fails to make the distinction between faith and belief.

Returning to the matter at hand, the Upanishads fall within the realm of scripture, part of the accumulated religious tradition of ancient India and therefore subject to change. Yet, they are sacred writings that have inspired faith and guided the lives of millions of human beings for millennia. The magic of scripture is its ability to inspire faith and recreate itself age after age and so reestablish its relevance from generation to generation. In this sense scripture is timeless. Why should these Upanishads be frozen to a certain time, the eighth century CE, and then only by one line of interpretation, Advaita Vedanta? Scripture belongs to the ages. I view the Upanishads as valuable and sacred works that also speak to our time and beyond India. They are the product of human theology as well as Hindu theology. They are relevant religious works that belong to the whole world as much as they belong to ancient India and Hinduism. Therefore, the present translation and annotations of these principal Upanishads have been largely made without recourse to any forms of *vedānta*, including Shankara's Advaita Vedanta. I wanted a fresh start. As the astronomer looks through a telescope and sees the light that has traveled for thousands of light years, similarly I wanted to look at the light of these Upanishads, see what they had to say in their time and then see what illumination they can provide us today, in our time and place, thousands of years since their inception.

Naturally, choosing to translate this way, consciously avoiding recourse to Indian traditions and commentators, creates certain limitation as well as advantages, and I am sure there will be criticism, particularly from devout Hindus who want to stay true to Hindu traditions. But there are hundreds of translations and studies that do precisely that. I direct my critics to them. This translation has been made by a Westerner who is also a practitioner. Given my Western perspective and knowing the distinction between faith and belief, I have tried to work with these sacred texts to find relevant meaning for who I am as a Westerner schooled in the West, but who is deeply involved in India and Hindu traditions. Being freed from the constraints of needing a *vedānta*, whether in the tradition of Shankara, Ramanuja or Madhva, allows me to look at these Upanishads in a new way.

What makes these Upanishads most valuable is their universal nature. They are generally non-sectarian and therefore outside of any particular religious tradition, even within India. They are not Vaishnavite, Shaivate, or part of the Shakta traditions. In general, no specific deity is mentioned as supreme. God remains unnamed. Of course, many deities and semi-divine beings are mentioned throughout the Upanishads. The sun, the moon, wind, rain are mentioned as deities. Many semi-divine beings, such as Gandharvas, are also mentioned. But when it comes to naming an ultimate being, God, no specific name is mentioned. Later Hindu traditions, which are sectarian in nature, glorify Vishnu, Shiva or Durga as that supreme Deity, but these principal Upanishads do not.

The main word for that Ultimate Source is *brahma,* and it is repeated over and over, but it is not the name of any specific deity. The word is neuter and is derived from the root *bṛh,* meaning to roar and expand. *Brahma* is ultimate power and force, and it is described as the substratum that underlies all existence and from which all things come and ultimately return. We also find words like *ātmā, puruṣa* and *īśa* being used to refer to that Supreme Source, but again they are not names. They are simply descriptions of that ultimate force and they respectively mean "supreme soul," "cosmic man" or "lord." Other such descriptive terms are also used, but never the name of a specific deity. This reluctance to impose the limitation of naming a specific deity is what gives the Upanishads their universal appeal. They are human yearnings for ultimate meaning and therefore a part of human religious thinking. Yes, they are part of the oldest Hindu traditions, but on a higher level they are not bound by geography and historical time, or even Hinduism itself. They are human and universal teachings.

These twelve principles Upanishads can be divided into three groups according to theme and historical development. The Brihad Aranyaka and the Chandogya Upanishads are what I call the sacrificial Upanishads. By "sacrificial" I mean Upanishads that focus on the Vedic *yajña* or *agni-hotra* fire ritual as their main emphasis. They are the oldest Upanishads. Next to them are the analytical Upanishads. These include the Taittiriya, Aitareya, Mandukya, Prashna, Mundaka, Kena, and the Katha Upanishads. By "analytical" I mean Upanishads that no longer build on the Vedic *yajña* as their theological foundation, but instead take an analytical approach in their teachings. The Taittiriya, for example, analyses the five *kośas* or "containers" that make up our existence in this physical world, our food container (*anna-maya-kośa*), our breath container (*prāṇa-maya-kośa*), our mental container (*mano-maya-kośa*), our intellect container (*vijñāna-maya-kośa*), and our joy container (*ānanda-maya-kośa*). The Mandukya Upanishad provides an analysis of four states of awareness, a waking state, a dream state, a deep sleep state, and a mystical state. The Mundaka Upanishad even criticizes Vedic ritual as inferior and just a distraction to the attainment of *brahma*. These analytical Upanishads appear after the sacrificial Upanishads. Later still are the Kaushitaki, Isha and the Shvetashvatara Upanishads, which are the devotional Upanishads as they offer prayers to that ultimate power *brahma* for salvation and protection in this world. They are the precursors of devotion (*bhakti*) best found in an even later work, the Bhagavad Gita, which is highly theistic in its devotion to Krishna.

There are a number themes running throughout the Upanishads that will be helpful in understanding these ancient works. The first is correspondence, that elements correspond to other elements. For example, the eye of God corresponds to the sun, which in turn corresponds to the eye of man. The breathing of God corresponds to the wind, which in turn corresponds to the breath within man. The mind of God corresponds to the moon, which in turn corresponds to the mind of man. The hairs on the body of God correspond to trees and vegetation, which in turn correspond to the hair on the body of man. Similar to this is the relationship between the macrocosm and the microcosm. The sun "up there" corresponds to a sun within man. The mars "up there" corresponds to a mars within man. In fact, this is the basis of Vedic astrology: Read the heavens "up there" and you can read the corresponding celestial bodies within man. The *ātmā* or soul of the cosmos corresponds to the soul within man. The *prāṇa* or life force of the cosmos is the life force within man. This theme of correspondence pervades the Shruti Vedas, and the Upanishads in particular.

Another related theme is the relationship between the whole and its parts. This famous verse from the Brihad Aranyaka (5.1.1) best captures this relationship:

*pūrṇam **adaḥ** pūrṇam **idam** pūrṇāt pūrṇam udacyate*
pūrṇasya pūrṇam ādāya pūrṇam evāvaśiṣyate

That is whole. **This** is whole. From wholeness, wholeness unfolds. Taking wholeness from wholeness, wholeness remains.

Here we see the use of two pronouns, *adas* and *idam*, "that" and "this." Looking out into the universe, the Upanishad says, "**That** is whole," the universe is whole. Then looking across this world, it says, "**This** is whole," this world is whole. Yet, in ordinary thinking we might say, yes, this universe is whole, but this world is just a part of that whole and therefore not whole. Yet here we are told that not only is the universe whole, the part is also whole! Then it goes on to say, take so many parts from this whole and still it remains whole! How can this be? If I have a whole pie and I take so many slices from that pie, the pie becomes smaller, incomplete. But here not only does the pie remain whole, the individual slices, the parts, are also whole. This implies that the whole is contained within the parts–that within every part of this world the whole is lying within. On another level the "that" refers to *brahma* (God) and the "this" refers to the individual *ātmā* or soul. Therefore, find the individual soul and you can find the universal soul. This is key to upanishadic thinking.

Another theme is *yajña*, sacrifice, particularly the fire sacrifice (*agni-hotra*). The two older Upanishads, the Brihad Aranyaka and the Chandogya, as we mentioned, especially focus on this ritual. In fact, the world is compared to an *agni-hotra*. The later primary Upanishads, the analytical upanishads move away from this theme and concentrate on less ritual matters of Hindu theology, but in this earliest period the *agni-hotra* is so important that it shapes the worldview of ancient Vedic culture. Simply put, the *agni-hotra* is about power. It was the overwhelming technology of the day. Creation took place with the help of the *agni-hotra*. This can clearly be seen in the opening chapters of both the Brihad Aranyaka and Chandogya Upanishads. The Brihad Aranyaka describes the world in terms of the horse sacrifice, the *aśva-medha-yajña*, which becomes a metaphor for the universe itself. The Chandogya Upanishad praises the power of sound and the mantras used in the *agni-hotra*. Both the gods and the demons use these rituals in the form of the High Chant, the *udgītha*, as they battle for control of the world.

The *agni-hotra* was an extremely elaborate and meticulous affair that was taken with absolute seriousness. In ancient times it was controlled by the priestly class, and it was so elaborate and costly that only the royal class and certain wealthy mercantile members had access to it. It conferred power, prestige and legitimacy on the royal order. Kings were coronated and given legitimacy by the priests using the *agni-hotra*. The fire sacrifice as we know it now is called a *havan* or *homa* depending on the region of India. It is still relevant and important in the daily lives of Hindus even as it has been democratized and made accessible to the common person. Today the *havan* or *homa* is a mere shadow of the *agni-hotra* as it was practiced in Vedic times. Hindu priests regularly perform these sacrifices in temples and the homes of Hindu families. Even though the fire sacrifice has been largely replaced by devotion it is still a significant part of Hindu religious life. In the days of the Upanishads, it was not just a part of the religious life—it **was** the religious life.

Another feature of the Upanishads is reductionism. What I mean by reductionism is the tendency to reduce life to its most basic level, the "nuts and bolts" of life, so to speak: breath, food, loneliness, power, etc. The Brihad Aranyaka and Chandogya Upanishads, for example, talk of food, breath, sex and power as the foundations of life. They even talk of loneliness as a reason for creation. God, *brahma*, felt alone and so, being alone and feeling the need for an other, creation burst forth. The very language of the Upanishads is simple and basic, yet sublime! Later Sanskrit texts like the Puranas have a much more embellished and flowery language involving complicated meters and word play, etc. The concepts and language of the Upanishads, however, are as simple and basic as language can be. And yet they are subtle and a delight to read!

There is a general understanding that the Upanishads only discuss the "high and mighty," which includes discussions of *brahma*, *ātmā* and *prāṇa,* God, the soul and life force. While this is certainly true, a lot more is discussed. A person who desires political power and progeny should perform the *agni-hotra* in a certain way. One who desires the destruction of enemies should also perform the *agni-hotra* according to certain rituals. A person who desires powerful sex should similarly perform the *agni-hotra*. One who desires the heavenly worlds wherein one can find unlimited pleasure can also follow the *agni-hotra* according to certain rituals.

The Upanishads are also full of geographic and historic references. Many times kings and priests come from various places to assemble for debate and wealth. The great King Janaka creates a contest wherein he entices the learned pundits of the day with the prize of cattle and gold. Yajnavalkya, the most learned scholar of his time, immediately comes and seizes the gold, to the horror of the other pundits. He boldly declares he is there for the gold. The Upanishads reflect human nature in all its forms, base and sublime. There are references to famine and drought and floods. There are references to social ideas involving caste, kings teaching *brāhmanas*, wealthy merchants and women receiving mystical knowledge, etc. There are references to female issues, including marriage, birth control and childbirth. There is misogyny. There is humor and satire. There is a section where priests are compared to chanting dogs barking for food and drink. And of course there is great poetry, and beautiful metaphors throughout. The honey talks from the Brihad Aranyaka Upanishad are exquisite.

These Upanishads show evidence of a religious shift. Joseph Campbell spoke of different religious types, namely religions of affirmation and religions of denial. Many early religions saw this world in positive terms. These are religions of affirmation and they tend to emphasize embracing and affirming the world as it is rather than seeking to escape it. An opposite religious mode is one of denial wherein the world is seen as blatantly evil, false and unreal. Such a religious view tends to focus on transcending or escaping the world of suffering and limitations. These religions often emphasize renunciation of worldly desires, ascetic practices, and detachment from material concerns. It is common within the same religious tradition to find these different phases of religious development at different times.

Within these principal Upanishads we can see evidence of religious affirmation in the earliest Upanishads with their emphasis on the Vedic sacrifice as a means to obtain whatever one desire in this world. Life was essentially good and the sacrifice was the means to contact the gods to obtain what was necessary to live happily. There was little concerns for salvation or release from this world. The Isha Upanishads tells us how to live a hundred years enjoying this world. It is a positive affirmation of life. But later on in the same principal Upanishads we can see a shift to a religion of denial. For example, the simple words *sat* and *asat* completely reverse their meaning from the early sacrificial Upanishads to the later devotional Upanishads thus suggesting a shift in religious type. The word *sat* literally means what is real and true. From *sat* we get the word *satya* which is generally translated as truth. *Asat* is the total opposite, what is unreal and untrue. In the later devotional Upanishads including works like the Bhagavad Gita, and throughout the *smriti* tradition, *sat* refers to God (*brahma*) and the soul (*ātmā*), whereas this physical world including the body are called *asat*, unreal and temporary. In other words, spiritual "things" are *sat* and physical "things" are *asat*. Yet in the early sacrificial Upanishads, especially the Brihad Aranyaka Upanishad *sat* is used to refer to this physical world while *asat* is used to refer to the unseen spiritual realm "up there" so to speak. And this makes good sense. This physical reality, what we see before us, **is** real. You can touch it, see it and walk on it. It is concrete and apparent, of course it is *sat*. On the other hand, the soul, God and a spiritual reality that may be "up there" or inside of us **is** unseen, intangible and elusive. It makes sense to call it *asat*. Referring to the world as *sat*, real and true, is an affirmation of the world. But the later shift to view the world as *asat*, unreal and false, is evidence of a religious shift from religious affirmation to religious denial. In its extreme form Advaita Vedanta uses the doctrine of illusion (*māyā*) to see this world as false and something to become free from.

The Upanishads are therefore much more than simply theological documents. They are historical works, they are literature, and, most important of all, they are human documents. They arose within India and are the product of Hindu thought, yet they easily rise to the level of world theology, world literature, and world scripture.

Brihad Aranyaka Upanishad

The Forest Teachings

Introduction to
Brihad Aranyaka Upanishad

The Brihad Aranyaka Upanishad, also known as the "Great Forest Upanishad," holds a prominent place among the principal Upanishads, which form the foundation of Hindu spiritual thought. The Brihad Aranyaka Upanishad forms the concluding section of the Shatapatha Brahmana of the White Yajur Veda and is thought to be the earliest of the principal Upanishads.

The Upanishad is comprised of six major sections called *adhyāyas*, which in turn are divided into chapters called *brāhmaṇas*. These six major sections are further grouped into three distinct parts, known as *kāṇḍas*. These *kāṇḍas* are named the Madhu Kanda, the "honey dialogues, the Yajnavalkya Kanda (also known as the Muni Kanda), questions and answers by the sage Yajnavalkya, and the Khila Kanda, a supplementary part that deals with an assortment of topics.

The Madhu Kanda (*adhyāyas* One and Two) explores the metaphysical concepts and philosophical inquiries regarding the nature of the ultimate reality. It delves into profound contemplations on the origin and nature of the universe, the Supreme Force (*brahma*), and the relationship between the individual self (*ātmā*) and the cosmic consciousness. Through intricate and poetic dialogues, it explores the nature of existence, creation, and the interconnectedness of all things.

The Yajnavalkya Kanda (*adhyāyas* Three and Four), often considered the core section of the Brihad Aranyaka Upanishad, focuses on the practical aspects of spiritual life and the pursuit of self-realization. This group is comprised of questions by various disciples and answers by the sage Yajnavalkya. It addresses various rituals, sacrifices, and meditative practices as means to attain spiritual enlightenment. It emphasizes the importance of self-discipline, meditation, and the cultivation of virtues such as truthfulness, compassion, and non-violence.

The Khila Kanda (*adhyāyas* Five and Six), comprises a collection of supplementary teachings and additional insights into various philosophical and ritualistic subjects. It explores diverse topics such as cosmology, the symbolic interpretations of rituals and many women's issues. While it may appear less structured than the preceding sections, it offers valuable insights and serves as a comprehensive source of knowledge for seekers of truth.

With its rich philosophical content, the Brihad Aranyaka Upanishad has had a significant influence on Hindu philosophy, spirituality, and religious practices. Its teachings have been widely studied, commented upon, and revered by scholars, seekers, and spiritual aspirants throughout history.

[1] This is a metaphor of the *aśva-medha,* the Horse Sacrifice, as the source of the world. One may question, why a horse? Why not an elephant or cow? To the ancient Aryans the horse and the chariot were the prime pieces of ancient war technology. It was the horse and chariot that allowed these Aryans to dominate. The horse remained a central symbol of royal power in ancient India, and the horse sacrifice that figures so prominently in this opening chapter of the Brihad Aranyaka Upanishad became the primary ritual expression of that power. Consequently, the Rig Veda is full of horse and chariot references. Later on other animals, such as the elephant and cow, took on significance, so today we associate elephants and cows as more Hindu than the horse. But in these early times the horse was king, so much so that in ancient India the *aśva-medha* was the most important and elaborate of Vedic sacrifices. It is described in detail in the *Shatapatha Brahmana* 13.1-5. In this sacrifice a king releases a horse to wander about at will for a year. Wherever that horse travels becomes the property of that king. If there is a dispute with a neighboring monarch, the soldiers, who follow the horse, fight to assert the sovereignty of their king. After a year, if the wanderings of the horse have been successful, the horse is sacrificed at a grand ceremony, the *aśva-medha,* and the king is consecrated as a universal monarch.

[2] The idea of a cosmic connection between a human body (or an animal body), the universe and a Supreme Being is a common Hindu theme that first appears in the Rig Veda (*Puruṣa Sukta* 10.90.129). There it describes how this universe is fashioned from the body of God: from the eye of God comes the sun, from the mind of God comes the moon, from the breathing of God comes the wind, etc. It is the idea that because this universe is fashioned from the body of God, it *is* the body of God. By extension it means there is a relationship between the macrocosm and the microcosm, between the whole and its parts. This understanding becomes the basis for Hindu astrology and even architecture, etc.

First *Adhyāya*

First *Brāhmaṇa*

The World as a Sacrificial Horse

1. Dawn is the head of the sacrificial horse.[1] The sun is its eye. Wind is its breath, and its wide open mouth is the universal fire.[2] The year is its body. The upper sky is its back; the lower sky is its stomach. The earth is its underbelly. Its sides are the directions, its ribs the intermediate directions. Its limbs are the seasons, and the months and the fortnights its joints. Day and night are the feet of this great horse. The stars are its bones, the clouds its flesh. Sand is the food in its belly. The rivers are its intestines, the hills its liver and lungs; plants and trees are its bodily hair. Its front is the rising sun, its back the setting sun. When this horse yawns, lightning flashes; when it shakes, there is thunder; when it urinates, there is rain. Its sound becomes speech.

2. The day is a sacrificial vessel placed before this horse.[3] Its location is the eastern ocean. The night is a sacrificial vessel placed behind this horse. Its location is the western ocean.[4] Indeed, these two sacrificial vessels arose on opposite sides of the horse. As a steed, it carries the gods; as a stallion, it carries the Gandharvas; as a racer, it carries the demons; and as a horse, it

---

[3] During the *aśva-medha* two vessels for libations are placed on either side of the horse, one of gold and the other of silver.

[4] This can be understood as the Arabian Sea on one side and the Bay of Bengal on the other side.

[5] The word is *bandhu*, a relation.
[6] The word is *yoni*, a womb. There is some interesting early symbolism here: the ocean as the source of life, which seems to agree with our modern idea that life evolved from the ocean.
[7] This is the first creation myth of the Upanishads and one of the earliest creation myths within Hinduism. An earlier Hindu myth appears in the Rig Veda (10.129), wherein it is stated that in the beginning "there was neither non-being nor being." In this version it is stated that "in the beginning there was not anything (*na... kiñcana*.)" Another version appears later in this Upanishad (BU 1.4) wherein it is stated that in the beginning there was only *ātmā*. Later on, in the CU, we will hear that in the beginning there was only non-being (*asat*) and that being (*sat*) came from this non-being. Then later, in the same CU, this view is refuted and it is stated that in the beginning there was being (*sat*) only. There are, in fact, many more creation myths throughout the Hindu tradition. The best way to understand this is by the dictum "If it is good, there should be more of it." Hinduism loves plurality. If God is good, there should be many. If one lifetime is good, there should be many lifetimes. In this present myth there is a subtle mixture of meanings. The words used here, *ātmā*, *arca*, *arka* and *kam,* all have multiple meanings, thus making the interpretation complex and subtle. The footnotes below will illustrate this complexity.
[8] This is the first usage of the word *ātmā* in the Upanishads. *Ātmā* is one of the most problematic and intriguing words to translate because of its multiple meanings. Its meaning must, therefore, be determined according to context. Sometimes *ātmā* is used in the sense of the Ultimate; therefore, such words as Soul, God, the Supreme Spirit, *brahma*, Self or even Lord can be employed. Other times, it is used in the sense of the individual; therefore, self, spirit, soul or one's self (as a reflexive pronoun) can be employed. And at other times it refers to the physical being of a person; therefore, breath, body, mind, intellect, life, nature, form, and even essence are appropriate. Here the best

carries men. Indeed, the ocean is its friend[5] and its source.[6]

Here ends the first *Brāhmaṇa* of the first *Adhyāya*

Second *Brāhmaṇa*

Creation

1. In the beginning there was nothing.[7] The world was desolate, covered by death and starvation alone. Indeed, starvation is death. Death thought, "Let me assume a form[8] and create a life." Death then roamed about performing action[9] and, as he did, water[10] appeared. Death then thought, "Action produces water. This gives me joy."[11]

---

contextual meaning seems to be in relation to physical being.

[9] Here the word is *arca*, which has two main meanings, to shine and to praise. We have translated it as action. This is a gloss, but what can also be meant is a type of liturgical recitation. Alternatively, this could be rendered as shining: "He roamed about shining." The word *arca* is also related to the word *arka*, used in the next sentence. *Arka* means light, but also can mean recitation. It is also a special kind of fire (light) used in the horse sacrifice, *aśva-medha.*

[10] The word here is *āpaḥ*, waters. In Sanskrit *āpaḥ* is always plural. Given the subtle wordplay in this section, it could be extended to include semen, thus introducing a sexual interpretation.

[11] The word used here is *kam*, which similarly has two meanings, joy and water. In other words, life arose! It is interesting that the root of the word *kam* is the same as for the word *kāma,* pleasure. This further suggests a sexual interpretation: that in moving about, water (semen) was produced, which gave death great joy. In another interpretation, sacrifice is physical work, and such work produces water in the form of sweat.

Action is illuminating. Indeed, joy comes to one who understands the illuminating nature of action.

2. Water is clear. This is its essence.[12] It darkened to form earth. Death continued to perform action and, as he labored, Death became hot from exertion. Heat is the essence of work.
It became fire.

3. Death divided himself threefold, as fire, sun and wind. He also divided his breath. His head became the east, his forequarters the northeast and southeast, his tail the west, and his two hindquarters the northwest and the southwest. His two sides became the north and the south. His back became the heavens, his underbelly the sky, and his chest the earth. In this way he established himself on earth.[13] One who understands this remains fixed in all situations.

4. He then considered, "I should have a second."[14] In his mind,

---

[12] The word is *rasa,* which can mean essence, water, or, again, even semen. Again, this strengthens the underlying sexual meaning.
[13] Literally, he stood firm on water.
[14] The word is *ātmā.*
[15] The word used here is *bhāṇ,* which is an onomatopoeia of a child's cry or breathing. It is also a verbal root meaning to sound or speak.
[16] *aditer aditiva*. The word *aditi* is derived from *ad,* to eat, the supreme eater, the all-consumer. It is often an epithet for God in the form of death. So this expression could also be translated as the "all-consuming nature of the Supreme."
[17] That is to say, he died.

Death joined with speech. His semen became the year. Before this there was no year. He bore this embryo for a year, after which he gave birth. As this child was born, Death opened his mouth to swallow it. And it cried out, "Stop!"[15]
This is how language arose.

5. He thought, "If I eat this one, I will have less food." So with speech and body he created this world and everything that exists, including the Rig, Yajur, and Sama Vedas, the meters, sacrifice, people and even beasts. Whatever he created, he began to eat. "He eats all things!"

This is the all-devouring nature of death.[16] One who knows the all-devouring nature of death himself becomes the eater of this world and all things become his food.

6. Death desired, "Let me perform sacrifice once again, but this time let it be an even greater sacrifice." He labored! He performed austerity and sacrifice until even splendor and power left him. Indeed, splendor and power are the life airs. So when his life airs departed, he began to swell.[17] Yet his mind remained within this body.

7. He desired, "I wish that my body could be sacrificed so that I may obtain another body. Thereupon it became the sacrificial horse. That which swells (*aśvat*) is the *aśva* and is fit for sacrifice" (*medhas*). This is why the horse sacrifice is called *aśva-medha*. One who knows the *aśva-medha* in this way truly understands.

Keeping the horse in mind, he let it run unrestrained for a year, after which he killed it as a sacrifice to himself. He offered other beasts to the gods. Therefore, a horse sacrificed to Prajāpati, the Lord of Creatures, is considered an offering for all the gods.

This sun that blazes up there is the *aśva-medha* sacrifice. The year is its body. The fire that burns down here is the fire of the

---

[18] Here the words *devas* (gods) and *asuras* (demons) are used. Both are offspring of the same father. Commentators suggest these two words refer to the organs of the body, including the mind. When these organs are disciplined they are gods (*devas*) and when they are undisciplined they are demons (*asuras*). Compare this to BG 6.5-6, where the mind is considered both a friend and an enemy. A similar version of this story also appears in CU 1.2.

[19] In this story the perennial struggle between good and evil is described.

[20] The word is *udgītha*, the High Chant. It is a most important portion of a Vedic *yajñā*, the fire sacrifice. The ritual generally has three main priests: a *hotṛ,* who chants hymns from the Rig Veda; an *adhvaryu,* who chants hymns from the Yajur Veda; and an *udgātṛ,* who chants hymns from the Sama Veda. It is this Sama priest who leads the *udgītha*. The whole first part of the CU focuses on this High Chant, *see* CU 1.1, CU 1.2, CU 1.3. Perhaps think of the High Chant as the most powerful technology of the day. Whichever side had access to this technology could dominate.

[21] In verses 2 through 6 the words *bhoga* and *kalyāna* reoccur. The word *bhoga* has been glossed as (sensual) pleasure, while *kalyāna* was been rendered as beauty. Pleasure was obtained for the bodily senses, the gods, while beauty was obtained for the *ātmā*. Here *ātmā* is glossed as a reflexive pronoun, but other meanings could be used as well. See BU 1.2.1 fn. The passage is therefore obscure.

aśva-medha. These worlds are its body. The sacrificial fire and the *aśva-medha* are two, yet they are one divinity: Death. The one who knows this no longer needs to be born. Death cannot seize him. Death becomes his body and he becomes himself one of the divinities.

Here ends the second *Brāhmaṇa* of the first *Adhyāya*

Third *Brāhmaṇa*

The High Chant
The Creation of Evil in the World
and the Superiority of Breath

1. The Lord of All Creatures, Prajapati, fathered both the gods and demons.[18] The gods were younger, the demons were older, yet they both competed for dominance in the world.[19]
The gods considered, "With the High Chant,[20] let us overcome the demons."

2. They approached speech and said,
"Sing the High Chant for us!"

"So be it!" Thereupon speech sang for them.

Whatever pleasure there is in speech was given to the gods. Whatever beauty there is in speaking it retained for itself.[21]
(The demons received nothing.)

The demons realized, "Using speech as the main chanter, the

gods will surely overcome us." So they rushed towards speech and pierced it with evil. Consequently, whatever falsehoods a person speaks come from this evil. Indeed, it makes a person evil.

3. The gods then spoke to the nose,[22]
"Sing the High Chant for us."

"So be it!" Thereupon the nose sang for them.

Whatever pleasure there is in breath was given to the gods. Whatever beauty there is as one smells it retained for itself. (The demons received nothing.)

The demons then realized, "Using the nose as the main chanter, the gods will surely overcome us." So they rushed towards the nose and pierced it with evil. Whatever disagreeable thing a person smells comes from this evil. Indeed, it makes a person evil.

4. The gods then spoke to the eye, "Sing the High Chant for us."

"So be it!" Thereupon the eye sang for them.

Whatever pleasure there is in sight was given to the eye.

---

[22] Here the word is *prāṇa,* which is literally breath. However, the use of the verb *ghrā,* to smell, in subsequent sentences suggests the actual meaning is the organ of smell, the nose. For more information see verse BU 1.3.7 and footnote where the word *prāṇa* is used as breath.

Whatever beauty there is in seeing was retained for itself.
(The demons received nothing.)

The demons then realized, "Using the eye as the main chanter, the gods will surely overcome us." So they rushed towards the eye and pierced it with evil. Whatever impure things a person sees come from this evil. Indeed, it makes a person evil.

5. The gods then spoke to the ear, "Sing the High Chant for us."

"So be it!" Thereupon the ear sang for them.

Whatever pleasure there is in sound was given to the gods.
Whatever beauty there is in hearing it retained for itself.
(The demons received nothing.)

The demons then realized, "Using the ear as the main chanter, the gods will surely overcome us." So they rushed towards the ear and pierced it with evil. Whatever falsehoods a person hears come from this evil. Indeed, it makes a person evil.

6. The gods then spoke to the mind,
"Sing the High Chant for us."

"So be it!" Thereupon the mind sang for them.

Whatever pleasure there is in thought was given to the gods.
Whatever beauty there is in imagination it retained for itself.
(The demons received nothing.)

The demons then realized, "Using the mind as the main chanter, the gods will surely overcome us." So they rushed towards the mind and pierced it with evil. Whatever bad things a person thinks come from this evil. Indeed, it makes a person evil.

---

[23] Literally, the expression is the "breath within the mouth" *(āsanyaṃ prāṇam).* Here this breath within the mouth has been translated as "main breath." In fact there are numerous breaths derived from this main breath. The general word for breath is *prāṇa*, but there are five derivative breaths: *prāṇa, apāna, vyāna, udāna* and *samāna.* The meaning of these five breaths has evolved over time and varies from text to text. This is the first reference to the word *prāṇa* in the Upanishads. From this point on, however, the word *prāṇa* will be used many times throughout this Upanishad and other Upanishads. It is a very significant and nuanced word, and so the meaning has to be determined by context. Sometimes the word *prāṇa* can even mean the senses and other vital functions of the body, such as blood circulation, ejaculation, menstruation, and even elimination.

[24] Compare this section to CU 1.2.7.

[25] The expression is *aṅgānām hi rasaḥ,* "the essence of the body." This is the Ayasya Angirasa who is mentioned below (BU 3.19) as the breath, which maintains all parts of the body.

[26] Ayasya Angirasa is the name of a Vedic *ṛṣi* cited in Rig Veda 10.67. He was a son of Angirasa and Svaraj, and was a famous Udgīthā or main chanter. He is associated metaphorically with breath, *prāṇa,* because breath is the most important bodily constituent and with breath one recites the Vedas.

[27] Dur, personified as a deity, is used as a name for the main breath in the mouth. The word *dūr* is derived from *dūra,* which means "distance" or "remote." In other words, the deity Dur can put death and evil at a distance.

In this way, the gods were attacked and pierced with evil.

7. The gods then spoke to the main breath,[23]
"Sing the High Chant for us!"

"So be it." Thereupon the main breath sang for them.

The demons then realized, "Using this main breath as the main chanter, the gods will surely overcome us." So they rushed towards breath to pierce it with evil. But like a clod of earth thrown against a rock, they were smashed and scattered in all directions. Thereupon the gods prospered and the demons declined. One who knows this will prosper, while his rivals, who are full of envy, will be ruined.[24]

8. The gods then asked, "Where did that main breath go?
He was so close to us."

"He is in the mouth! He is the very essence of the body.[25]
He is Ayasya Angirasa.[26]

9. "Death cannot harm this main breath; it stays far away from him. For this reason this main breath is called Dur."[27]
Therefore death stays away from one who understands this.

10. Indeed, this god, Dur, pushed back the evil of death from the other gods and chased it to the outer limits, where it deposited its evil. Therefore, one should not travel to foreign lands where one will find evil and death.

11. Having protected the gods from this deathly evil,
Dur carried them all away from death.

12. Speech was the first to be carried from death. Being freed from death, speech became fire. Transcending death, fire burns brightly in this world.

13. It then carried the nose. Being freed from death, the nose became the wind. Transcending death, the wind blows and purifies this world.

14. It then carried the eye. Being freed from death, the eye became the sun. Transcending death, the sun blazes forth.

---

[28] The word is *āgayāt*, from the root *gai*, to sing. The meaning could be Breath began to sing or chant the Vedas. I have taken it as "breathe." Breath began to breathe. Breathing and eating are two of the most essential functions that sustain life, and this is recognized.

[29] The Sanskrit is *iha pratitiṣṭhati*, which literally means "it stands firm here." The implied meaning is that food is the foundation of this world and that the ultimate eater of food is breath or life itself. In other words, life is food for life. This is a fixed principle of this world.

[30] As this one in the mouth, Breath, ate, all the gods were nourished. In other words, feed the whole and all the parts are automatically included. Water the roots of a tree and all the leaves and branches are automatically nourished.

[31] Here there is a play on words. As noted above in a previous footnote, Ayasya Angirasa is the name of a well-known seer associated with breath. The word *Angirasa* is derived from *āṅga* (bodily parts) and *rasa* (the essence). This breath is what gives life to all parts of the body.

15. It then carried the ear. Being freed from death, the ear became the directions. Indeed, they too transcended death.

16. It then carried the mind. Being freed from death, the mind became the moon. Transcending death, the moon shines in this world. Similarly, this deity carries anyone away from death who understands this.

17. To sustain this world Breath then began to breathe[28] and acquire food. Indeed, Breath consumes all things in this world and so stands supreme.[29]

18. The gods then spoke, "Whatever exists in this world is but food, and you have acquired it through breathing. Share some with us."

Breath called them, "Gather around."

"Yes!" And they gathered around Breath. Whatever food he ate satisfied them all.[30] Thus, one who understands this principle gathers around Breath as the leader, the master, the lord, and the supreme eater of food. But in spite of knowing this, a person who wants to rival this deity will never be able to support even his own dependents. On the other hand, the person who follows this principle will easily support his dependents.

19. This main breath is Ayasya Angirasa.[31] Indeed, Breath is the essence of the body. Say it again: Breath is the essence of the body. So, from whatever part Breath steps away, that part

[32] The word *bṛhat* means great and *pati* means lord.
[33] The word is *vāk,* which means speech, and she is seen as a goddess.
[34] This Brihad Aranyaka Upanishad is generally considered to be the oldest and therefore the first Upanishad. This is the first use of the word *brahma* in all the Upanishads. *Brahma* is also the last word used in this Upanishad. *Brahma* is an important and also problematic word. In fact, three words are problematic in the Upanishads, *brahma*, *ātmā* and *prāṇa,* because they all have multiple meanings which can only be interpreted contextually. Along with other features of Sanskrit grammar, this creates huge variations in interpretation, which is partly why there are many schools of theological interpretation within Hinduism. Grammatically, the stem of the word *brahma* is *brahman,* which can be either neuter or masculine. How this word is interpreted, as masculine or neuter, makes a huge difference in interpretation. As a neuter word, *brahman* becomes *brahma* and means the supreme force, i.e., God in an impersonal way, if you will. It can also mean the Vedas. *Brahman* as a masculine word is declined as *brahmā* and it means the creator god, Brahmā, part of the trinity of Brahmā, Vishnu, and Shiva common in later Hinduism. There is some question whether Brahmā, the creator god, is ever referred to at all in this Upanishad. Some commentators think so, others do not. In this particular case most commentators take *brahman* here as neuter, so to mean the chanted mantras of the Vedas.
[35] The feminine pronoun *sā* and the masculine pronoun *ama* combine to make the word *sāman.* The word suggests that the *sāman* encompasses both male and female, i.e., all things.
[36] The word *sāma* can also be derived from *sama. Sama* means "equal," so that which is based on *sama* is *sāma, i.e., sameness* or *equality.* Here the idea is that *brahma* is both the tiniest of things as well as the biggest of things. Again, the idea is that *brahma* is all things.

withers. Breath, indeed, is the essence of the body!

20-21. This Breath is Brihaspati,[32] the Great Lord. It is also the Brahmanaspati, the Lord of speech.[33] He is her lord; therefore he is known as Brahmanaspati.[34]

22. This breath is the *sāman*. *Sāman* is speech. "It is both she (*sā*) and he (*ama*).[35] Or because it is equal to all things, a gnat, a mosquito, an elephant, the three worlds, or even the entire universe, it is called *sāman*.[36] One who understands this gains intimacy with and dwells in the same world as the *sāman*.

23. This Breath is also the High Chant, the *udgītha,* and because it is both high (*ut*) and a chant (*gīthā*) it is called the *udgītha*.

24. While drinking King Soma,[37] Brahmadatta Caikitāneya has said, "If Ayasya Angirasa sang by any other means, may King Soma shatter my head."[38] Only with speech and breath did he sing the *udgītha*.

25. One who understands the best quality of the *sāman* comes to possess that quality. Indeed, musical tone[39] is that best quality.

---

[37] The text simply says *rāja*, king. Commentators suggest it means King Soma, the elixir pressed from the soma plant. The verse is obscure.

[38] This reference to shattering or bursting of a head is similar to the modern day expression "blows the mind."

[39] The word is *svara*, tone.

Therefore, when one chants one should wish for a tone in his voice. Possessing that tone, let him chant. During a sacrifice people only want to hear a priest who possesses that quality. Therefore, one who knows this quality of *sāman* comes to possess this quality.

26. This is the wealth of *sāman*, and one who knows this comes to possess this wealth. Indeed, tone is that wealth. One who understands will gain gold.

27. One who understands the foundation of *sāman* himself gains a foundation. Voice is that foundation. Breath, being established in voice, sings. Others say that food is the foundation.

28. Next begins the recitation of the purificatory hymns known as the *pavamānas*.[40] As the priest chants, the patrons should silently recite:

---

[40] The *pavamāna* hymns, also known as the *bahiṣpavamāna* hymns, are a set of liturgical hymns sung at a Soma sacrifice. For further reference see CU 1.12.14

[41] This is the famous *asato gamaya* verse, known as the three *pavamāna* mantras. This is also the first usage of the word *sat* in the Upanishads. For further uses see footnotes under BU 1.6.3 and 2.3.1. It is interesting to note that while all the focus on ritual perfection has largely been eclipsed, these three mantras live on and are still recited in popular Hinduism.

[42] This is the second creation myth of this Upanishad.

[43] Here the contextual meaning of *ātmā* suggests some form of the Ultimate. See Footnote under BU 1.2.1.

[44] Literally, the word *puruṣa* is "man." Here we can take it as "cosmic man."

From the unreal lead me to the real (*asato mā sad gamaya),*
From darkness lead me to light (*tamaso mā jyotir gamaya*),
From death lead me to immortality[41]
(*mrityor māmritam gamaya).*

When it says *asato mā sad gamaya*, "from the unreal lead me to the real," death is the unreal, immortality is the real. "From death lead me to immortality" means make me immortal. When it says "From darkness lead me to light," death is darkness, immortality is light. In the expression *mrityor māmritam gamaya*, "from death lead me to immortality," there is nothing difficult in these words.

Therefore, let him chant the other verses to obtain a living for himself. Let him choose a boon, whatever he desires. By chanting verses a priest may obtain for himself or his patron whatever he wishes. This indeed is world conquest! In this way, for one who knows the *sāman* there is never a fear of being without a conquered realm.

Here ends the third *Brāhmaṇa* of the first *Adhyāya*

Fourth *Brāhmaṇa*

The Creation[42]

1. In the beginning this world was only *ātmā*[43] in the form of *puruṣa.*[44] Looking around, It saw nothing other than Itself. It then uttered, "I am." Immediately, the word "I" appeared. Therefore, even today, when one is called, one first answers "It is I" followed by one's name.

2. It was afraid. Therefore, one who is alone fears. But It noticed, "Since nothing exists other than Me, whom should I fear?" Thereupon fear vanished. If one is alone, should one be afraid? Indeed, it is only from a second that fear arises.

3. But It had no joy. One who is alone has no joy. It therefore desired a second. It so happened that It was as large as a woman and a man combined in an embrace. It therefore split itself into two parts. Thereupon arose a husband and a wife.[45] Because of

---

[45] Here the words are *pati* and *patnī*.

[46] Out of shame she hid herself.

[47] *srithyām ha etasya etasyām bhavati*, literally "Indeed, he becomes a part of this creation."

[48] The verb *amantha,* from the root *manth*, means to churn or rub. When it is used with *agni* (fire), it refers to rubbing a stick (a fire-drill) to produce fire.

[49] The word is *yoni*, which literally is the female organ. A *yoni* is also the opening to a container that holds the sacrificial fire, a *havana kuṇḍa.* Here the reference is to the mouth, which, like the opening to the sacrificial container, can also produce fire. The meaning is by rubbing his hands together and blowing air from his mouth he produced fire.

[50] There is an obvious sexual meaning here. Fire is power, it is life, so by moving the hands together, blowing from the mouth and rubbing the stick, one produces fire, which is life. In the same way, from the rubbing during copulation, life is produced.

[51] The word "nectar" is *soma. Soma* is a kind of sacred beverage extracted and consumed during a ritual. Even though there are many hymns and descriptions of this *soma,* it is not clear what this elixir was.

this Yājnavalkya has said, "One's self is only half." Therefore, this other half is filled by woman. He joined with her and human beings were created.

4. But then this woman thought, "He joins with me after he has produced me from himself![46] Come, let me hide." She became a cow. He became a bull. He joined with her. Cattle were born. She became a mare, he a stallion. She became a she-ass, he a male-ass. He joined with her. Solid-hoofed animals were born. She became a female goat, he a male goat; she an ewe, he a ram. He again joined with her. Goats and sheep were born. In this way all things were created in pairs, even down to the ants.

5. It then thought, "Indeed, I am this creation; I produced it all!" So this is how creation arose, and one who knows this prospers.[47]

6. It then began to rub.[48] It produced fire from Its mouth using Its hands like a fire spout.[49] For this reason both one's hands and mouth are without hair. So also is the inside of the female organ.[50]

People say: "Worship this god; perform sacrifice to that god. One god after another, perform worship." Indeed, this is the way of creation for this One created the gods.

Whatever is moist and fresh in this world has been created from Its semen. It is nectar.[51] Indeed, everything in this world is just food and its eater. Nectar is the food and fire is the eater.

This world is the superb creation of *brahma:*[52] Behold, It created the gods, who are superior, and even though It is mortal Itself, It created the immortals! Therefore, this is an extraordinary cre-

---

[52] Some commentators take this as a reference to the creator god Brahmā. See BU 1.3.21 footnote for more explanation. Other commentators take it as Prajapati, which is often another name for the creator god Brahmā. Here we have taken it as a neuter noun, *brahma,* and not as a masculine noun, Brahmā.

[53] Literally, "One who knows this exists within his super-creation."

[54] Here the word is *avyākrīta,* which means undeveloped, but it can also refer to "an elementary substance from which all things are created."

[55] Here the expression *viśvambharo vā viśvambhara-kulāye* is obscure. *Viśvambhara* is literally all-bearing or all-sustaining and could refer to the all-pervading spirit sometimes identified with Vishnu or Indra. But the word also is a kind of insect, similar to a termite or scorpion. *Kulāya* is a receptacle, a nest, a resting place, which here could mean the body or even the universe itself. So the expression could refer to the supreme spirit who resides in every inch of this universe or to a termite in its nest. Some translators even render the expression as "fire in a fire-holder." The overall idea, however, is clear: It refers to the invisibility of something which is encased.

[56] Literally, he is incomplete or not whole (*akritsna*) in any one of these things.

[57] The word is *padanīya*, which the dictionaries render as "to be investigated." The literal meaning is "to be footed towards."

[58] The word is *antaratama*, which also may be taken as the "innermost" thing.

[59] In other words, you will lose it.

ation. And one who knows this prospers.[53]

7. In the beginning everything was undeveloped.[54] It gradually became distinguished by name and form. So we say "This person has this name and he has this form." In this way the whole world is divided into name and form, and we say "He has this name, he has this form."

It enters this body to the very nail tips, just like a razor sits perfectly in its razor case or as a termite resides in its nest.[55] No one can see It, because It never appears whole. When breathing, It is perceived as breath; when speaking, It is perceived as speech; when seeing, It is perceived as sight; when hearing, It is perceived as sound; and when thinking, It is perceived as thought. Yet these are only the names of Its various activities.

One who considers It to be any of these things alone does not understand, for It cannot be perceived in these things individually.[56] One should consider these things collectively to be the *ātmā*, for this is where they are one. This *ātmā* is the trail[57] to all things, for through it all things can be known, just as by following their footprints one can find the cattle. One who knows this gains fame and glory.

8. This *ātmā* is more dear than a son, more dear than wealth, and more dear than all other things because it is the closest.[58] If a person thinks something else is more dear, one can safely say "You will cry."[59] Indeed, it will happen. One should revere the *ātmā* alone as most dear for he will never lose it.

9. Men often think that through knowledge of *brahma* they will become the whole. So what is it that *brahma* knew by which It became the whole?

10. In the beginning this world was *brahma* alone. It knew only Itself and so thought "I am *brahma.*" In this way It was all things. Amongst the gods, whoever realized this also became this whole, and likewise for sages (*ṛṣis*) and human beings. In

---

[60] This is a reference to RV 4.26.1. Vamadeva is the Rishi of the fourth book of the Rig Veda.

[61] This is an interesting observation on the effect of this kind of knowledge and the loss of innocence. This is reminiscent of the biblical story of Adam biting into the apple of knowledge and thereby losing his innocence.

[62] The verb used here is *vi-bhū*, which means to manifest, to arise or appear. The negative particle, *na*, which precedes, negates it.

[63] "Ruling power" is a translation of *kṣatra*, which means dominion, power or supremacy. The *kṣatriyas* are the class who manifest this power and they are the second of the four *varṇas* that form the basis of the later Hindu caste system. The four *varṇas* include *brāhmana*, *kṣatriya*, *vaiśya* and *śūdra,* who are sometimes viewed as the head, arms, belly and feet of the social body.

[64] A coronation ceremony is the *rājasuya* ritual in ancient India.

[65] "The priestly class" is a translation of *brāhmana*, literally "the knowers of *brahma*." The *brāhmanas* are therefore *brahma* made human in this world.

[66] This relationship between royal power and religious power has been reflected throughout the history of India as the relationship between *brāhmanas* and *kṣatriyas,* or in the West between church and state, i.e., religious power and political power.

the past the sage Vamadeva realized this and declared, "I am man, I am the sun."[60] Indeed, this is true even today. So one who understands "I am *brahma*" becomes this whole, and even the gods are powerless to stop one thus situated. For he is their very *ātmā*.

So when one venerates another divinity and not the *ātmā* and thinks "He is one and I am another," that person does not understand. As an animal is to a man, so man is to the gods. As a man enjoys having many animals, so man is enjoyed by the gods. And just as the loss of even one animal is not enjoyable to a man, so much more is the loss of many animals. Similarly, the gods are not pleased when men come to understand this.[61]

11. In the beginning this world was only *brahma* and, being alone, it was without form.[62] *Brahma* then created something better than Itself in the form of ruling power,[63] which manifests among the gods as Indra, Varuna, Soma, Rudra, Parjanya, Yama, Mrityu, and Isana. Nothing is higher than this ruling power. Therefore, in a royal coronation[64] the priestly class[65] sits lower and venerates the royal order. Yet the *brāhmana* blesses the royal order. Indeed, *brahma* is the source of the royal order. So whenever a king ascends to the throne, he ultimately needs the blessing of the *brāhmana* as the source of his power. Therefore, a king who harms a priest attacks his very source and degrades himself to the degree that he has harmed this one who is his better.[66]

12. *Brahma* was still not developed, so it created mercantile

power, which became manifest among the gods as the Vasus, the Rudras, the Adityas, the Vishvadevass, and the Maruts.[67]

13. Still *brahma* was not fully developed, so It created the working class as *pūṣan*,[68] the earth that nourishes all things.

14. Yet still *brahma* was not fully developed, so It created some-

---

[67] There are eight Vasus: fire, earth, wind, atmosphere, sun, sky, moon, and the stars. Fire is their mouth. There are eleven Rudras, of which Shiva is the principle. The sun is given a different name in each month. Therefore there are twelve suns known as the Twelve Adityas. The Vishvadevas are a class of divine beings, ten in number. They are the sons of Vishva. The Maruts are the storm gods, of which there are forty-nine. Marici is the head.

[68] *Pushan* is a Vedic deity sometimes associated with the earth and sometimes with the sun. Literally the word is derived from *puṣ,* "to nourish," and so it means "one who nourishes."

[69] The word *dharma* is derived from the Sanskrit root *dhṛ,* meaning to hold up, to carry, to bear, to sustain. Human society, for example, is sustained and upheld by the *dharma* performed by its members. Parents protecting and maintaining children, children being obedient to parents, a king protecting the citizens are all *dharmas* that uphold and sustain society. In these contexts *dharma* has the meaning of duty. *Dharma* also employs the meaning of law, religion, virtue, and ethics. These things uphold and sustain the proper functioning of human society. In philosophy *dharma* refers to the defining quality of an object. For instance, liquidity is one of the essential *dharmas* of water, coldness is a *dharma* of ice. In this case we can think that the existence of an object is sustained and defined by its essential attributes, *dharmas*.

[70] The verb is *samāśams*, to adjudicate.

thing even better, *dharma,*[69] which is the power of the royal order. Therefore nothing is superior to *dharma*. It is by *dharma* the weak overcome[70] the strong, by appealing to a king. Indeed, *dharma* is nothing but truth. So they say when a person speaks truth he speaks *dharma* and when he speaks *dharma* he speaks truth. In fact, both are the same.

15. In this way, *brahma* became manifest as *brāhmana, kṣatriya, vaiśya* and *śūdra* power. Among the gods *brahma* appeared as fire. In the human world it became the priestly order. As *kṣatriya* power it became the royal order, as *vaiśya* power it became the mercantile community, and as *śūdra* power it became the working class. Therefore people desire a place among the gods through fire and a place within the human world through the *brāhmana*. Starting from these two, *brahma* became manifest in this world.

Yet one who does not know this, who departs this world without recognizing his own position, cannot prosper, just as the Vedas unstudied or a deed undone gives no benefit. Indeed, if someone performs a deed that can give great benefit, yet he fails to understand this knowledge, that benefit will not endure. One should recognize *ātmā* alone as the Real. For one who recognizes *ātmā*, his deeds do not diminish because from *ātmā* he creates whatever he desires.

16. As *ātmā* is the object of enjoyment for all beings, so the one who sacrifices and makes offerings is the object of enjoyment for the gods. As one who recites the Vedas is the object of en-

joyment for sages, so one who offers libations to ancestors and desires offspring is the object of enjoyment for ancestors. As one who provides food and shelter to men is the object of enjoyment for them, so one who finds fodder and water for livestock becomes the object of enjoyment for them. When beasts and birds, even down to the ants, find life in a person's home, he becomes the object of enjoyment for them. Just as you desire enjoyment and security in your world, so all beings desire enjoyment and security in their world. Indeed, this is known upon reflection.

17. In the beginning this world was *ātmā* alone. It desired, "If I had a wife, I could procreate. I should have wealth, then I could do good things." How great indeed is desire! Even if one desires one cannot find more than this. So even today, if one is alone he desires, "I should have a wife, then I could procreate. I should have wealth, then I could do good things." To the degree a man has not obtained these things, he feels incomplete. The complete state of being is as follows: Mind is the *ātmā*, speech is the wife, breath is the offspring. The eye is human wealth, for with the eye one finds worldly wealth. The ear is divine wealth, for through the ear one hears divine wealth.[71] The body is action,

---

[71] Spiritual knowledge is divine wealth, which is gained through aural reception, hearing. Therefore, the ears are the source of divine wealth.

[72] As before, this can be taken as *agni-hotra* (fire sacrifice).

[73] Here the word is *paśu*, the sacrificial animal.

[74] Literally, "The one who knows this obtains this world."

[75] The word used here is *pitā*, "father," which implies Prajapati, the lord of creatures.

for with the body one performs good work.[72] Sacrifice is fivefold. The object of sacrifice[73] is fivefold. A person is fivefold. Indeed, this whole world is fivefold. One who knows this prospers.[74]

Here ends the fourth *Brāhmaṇa* of the first *Adhyāya*

Fifth *Brāhmaṇa*

Seven Kinds of Food

1. There are the following verses:

Through knowledge and austerity
The creator produced seven kinds of food:
One common to all,
Two apportioned for the gods,
Three for himself, and
One for beasts.
All beings depend on food,
Both those who breathe and those who do not.

Being constantly eaten,
Why is the supply of food never diminished?

One who understands
the inexhaustibility of food eats in plenty.
He goes to the gods and lives with vitality.

2. "Through knowledge and austerity the creator[75] produced

seven kinds of food" means that, through intelligence and hard work, Prajapati, the lord of beings, produced food.

"One common to all" refers to the food that is commonly eaten in this world. One who eats this food is never freed from evil, for this food is mixed.[76]

"Two apportioned for the gods" refers to both cooked and uncooked offerings.[77] Therefore people offer both to the gods. Yet others say these two are the new moon and the full moon sacrifices. Regardless, one should never perform sacrifice with a desire for gain.

---

[76] The word for evil is *pāpa.* Here the expression is *pāpmān*, possessed of *pāpa*. This means that such food is mixed with this evil. The idea is that food not first offered to *brahma* through sacrifice is tainted with this *pāpa*. See fn. 77.

[77] The words are *huta* and *prahuta*. There is debate on what this means. Some say *huta* is cooked food that is offered into the fire and *prahuta* is uncooked food that is offered into the fire. Others say *huta* is any food offered into the fire and *prahuta* is *prasada*, food left over after sacrifice. Another view is that *huta* is food offered to gods and *prahuta* is food offered to *brāhmanas*. The larger point is that food offered in sacrifice to *brahma* becomes free from *pāpa*.

[78] Which is to say he does not have to sacrifice for a full year to get the result.

[79] This could also be read as "For he offers all his food to the gods."

[80] As *brahma* is inexhaustible, so everything coming from *brahma* is inexhaustible, including the food supply.

[81] This simply means he eats to his full satisfaction.

"One for beasts" means milk for both men and animals. Milk is food taken in infancy. Therefore, as soon as a child is born it is allowed to lick some butter or suckle from the breast. Similarly, when a calf is born it does not eat grass.

"All beings depend on food, both those who breathe and those who do not" means that all this world depends on milk. In this regard, there are those who declare that one who performs sacrifice with milk for a full year overcomes repeated death. However, this should not be accepted because on the very day a learned person performs the sacrifice he overcomes death,[78] for he offers the whole world to the gods as food.[79]

"Why is the supply of food never diminished" means that the Supreme Person is inexhaustible and is constantly producing more food.

"One who understands this inexhaustibility" means the Supreme Person is inexhaustible and, through constant attention and work, He is producing an inexhaustible supply of food, and if He ceased to work all food would diminish.[80]

"Eats in plenty" means he eats through the mouth.[81]

"He goes to the gods and lives with vitality" is praise.

3. "Three were made for himself" refers to mind, speech and breath. These he made for himself. "I did not see it, my mind was elsewhere." "I did not hear it, my mind was elsewhere."

For indeed, it is with the mind that one sees, and it is with the mind that one hears! Desire, imagination, doubt, faith, lack of faith, determination, lack of determination, shame, thoughtfulness, fear, all these arise in the mind. Therefore, even when we are touched on the back we perceive it in the mind.

Speech, which is fashioned from basic sound, is defined by an object, whereas sound is not dependent on anything.[82]

Breath has the following constituents: *prāṇa*, *apāna*, *vyāna*, *udāna*, and *samāna*.[83] Together these, along with mind, speech and breath, constitute our physical existence.

4. From these the three worlds arise: The world here is speech, the middle atmosphere world is mind, and the higher world is breath.

5. From these the three Vedas arise: Speech is the Rig Veda, mind is the Yajur Veda, and breath is the Sāma Veda.

---

[82] Speech is speech because it has a referent, whereas sound is not bound by any object. Similarly, this world is fashioned from *brahma*, yet *brahma* is not defined by this world.

[83] The meaning of these technical terms varies, but a good explanation is as follows: *Prāṇa* is the vital energy that enters the body through breathing and is sent to every cell through the circulatory system. *Apāna* is the elimination of waste products from the body through the lungs and excretory systems. *Uḍāna* is sound production through the vocal apparatus, as in speaking, singing, laughing, and crying. *Samāna* is the digestion of food and cell metabolism. *Vyāna* is the expansion and contraction processes of the body, such as the circulatory system.

6. From these the gods, the ancestors and mankind arise: The gods are speech, the ancestors are mind, and mankind is breath.

7. From these father, mother, and offspring arise: Mother is speech, father is mind, and offspring are breath.

8-10. From these what is known, what is desired to be known, and what is unknown arise. Whatever is known is a form of speech. Knowing brings one closer to speech. The desire to know is a form of mind. For the desire to know is the function of the mind. Understanding this brings one closer to mind. Whatever is not known is a form of breath. For breath is what is not known. Understanding this brings one closer to breath.

11. Speech's body is the earth. Fire is its illumination. As far as speech extends, so does earth and fire.

12. Similarly, the mind's body is the sky. The sun is its illumination. As far as mind extends, so does the sky and the sun. These two joined in sexual union and breath was born. He was Indra and he was without a rival. There must be a second in order for there to be a rival. One who knows this will never be rivaled.

13. Similarly, breath's body is water. The moon is its illumination. As far as breath extends, so does water and the moon.

These are all equal. All are infinite. Yet one who understands them as finite gains a finite world, whereas one who understands them as infinite gains an infinite world.

The Lord of Creatures as the Year

14. The Lord of Creatures, Prajapati, became the year comprised of sixteen parts. His nights are fifteen parts. Firmness alone is his sixteenth part. With the passing of each night he is increased and he is decreased (he waxes and wanes). On that new moon night he enters all this that breathes and is again born that next morning. Therefore, in honor of the divine, one must not harm any being that lives on that night, not even a lizard.

15. Indeed, the person who knows this becomes like that Lord of Creatures, who is the year composed of sixteen parts. Wealth and power are his fifteen parts. His body[84] is his sixteenth part. In wealth and power one increases and decreases. That which is the center of this wheel is the body. Wealth and power are the outer rim of the wheel. Therefore, if someone is overcome by the total loss of wealth, if he still has his body, they say he has only lost his outer part.

---

[84] Here the word is *ātmā.* This could also be taken as mind or soul.

[85] There is a similar Prayer of Transference found in the Kaushitaki Upanishad 2.15.

[86] The word here is *prāṇa,* and in this context it means speech, mind and breath.

[87] Manu Samhita 9/138: Because a son delivers (*trayate*) his father from the hell called *pu*, a son is therefore called *putra* by the Self-existent Lord, Svayambhu.

The Three Worlds

16. Indeed, there are but three worlds: the world of man, the world of ancestors, and the world of the gods. One achieves success in the world of man through a son alone. One achieves success in the world of ancestors through sacred rites, and one achieves success in the world of the gods through knowledge. For this reason the world of the gods is best and is the most glorified.

The Rite of Transference

17. Now the Rite of Transference.[85] When a man knows he is about to depart this world, he should say to his son, "You are *brahma*, you are *yajñā*, and you are *loka*."

The son replies, "Yes, I am *brahma*, I am *yajñā*, I am *loka*." The sum total of all learning is what is meant by *brahma*. The sum total of all that has been sacrificed in life is what is meant by *yajñā*. The sum total of all things gained in life is what is meant by *loka*. *Brahma*, *yajñā* and *loka* comprise all things.

"Being the embodiment of all these things, let this son now assist me from this world." Therefore, it is said, an educated son is world-procuring. For this reason people educate their sons.

When a man of learning departs this world, he enters his son through these vital faculties.[86] Therefore, whatever has been done improperly throughout a life, a son frees his father from these things. Consequently, a son is called *putra*.[87] Through a son a father prospers.[88] In this way divine faculties enter a man, who assigns his mortal faculties to a son.

18. From earth and fire divine speech enters this man. Indeed, whatever is uttered through this divine speech comes to be.

19. From the heavens and the sun divine mind enters this man. It is through divine mind that he becomes joyful and never sorrows.

20. From waters and the moon divine breath enters this man. This divine breath, whether moving or unmoving, is never disturbed or injured in any way. One who knows this becomes the soul of all beings.

As that divinity is, so he is. As all beings favor that divine one, so they also favor one who knows that divine one. Whatever suffering afflicts these beings remains with them. Good alone goes to this one. Evil never goes to the gods.

---

[88] Literally, he "stands firm."

[89] Here the expression is *madhyama prāṇa,* which is literally "the middle breath," the breath that is held between inhalation and exhalation.

[90] Indeed, the meaning of the word *prāṇa* often extends to include the senses and other vital functions.

[91] The word is *adhyātmā*, where *ātmā* is taken as the physical body.

The Competition of the Senses

21. Now an examination of the vital functions. Prajāpati, the lord of creatures, created the senses. Once created, they began to compete with each other.

Speech declared, "I am going to speak!"

The eye shot back, "No, I am going to see!"

The ear declared, "No, I am going to hear!"

In this way each of the senses spoke. But then death, in the form of fatigue, took hold of them and blocked their functions. Therefore, speech became weary, the eye became weary, and the ear became weary. Yet death could not take hold of breath.[89] So they desired to know breath. "He is definitely better! Whether moving or not moving, he is never disturbed or hurt. Let us all become like him." So the senses became forms of him. Therefore they are also called "breaths."[90] In this way a family is named after a man who knows this, and anyone who competes with him in the end withers away and dies. All this is in reference to the body.[91]

22. Now let us regard the matter as it pertains to the divinities.

Fire called out, "I will blaze forth!"

The sun retorted, "I will burn hot!"

The moon spoke, "I will shine bright." Similarly, the other divinities declared according to their powers. Yet as breath was amongst the vital functions of the body, so the wind is amongst the divinities. The divinities diminished, but the wind did not. The wind is the only divinity who does not diminish.

23. In this regard there is a verse:

From where does the sun rise and where does it set?
It is from breath that it rises and into breath that it sets.
This is the law the gods have fashioned.

---

[92] Verses 22 and 23 again show the equivalency between the macrocosm and the microcosm. Air on the outside is wind. Air on the inside is breath.

[93] The word here is *uktham*, which is literally "a hymn of praise." Given the context, it has been glossed as "source."

[94] Here the word used is *brahma*, which has been rendered as "foundation" in this verse and the next two.

[95] What has been translated as "the Real" is a rendering of *sat.* The word *sat* refers to what is real, what is tangible, and what is true. So here *sat* refers to this threefold world of name, form, and action because this world is perceived as real, tangible, and true. In later Hinduism *sat* refers to God and soul (*brahma* and *ātmā*), and not to this world. Instead, *asat* is the word used to refer to this world. Only God and soul are real, while this world is unreal and illusory. See BG 2.16. This is the complete opposite to the usage here. In this early form of Upanishadic Hinduism the world of name and form is seen as real, tangible, and true, and therefore is called *sat.* For a similar usage see BU 2.1.20, 2.3.1 and 5.5.1.

It is this way today and it will be this way tomorrow.

What the gods did in the past they continue to do today. Therefore one should make a single vow while breathing in and breathing out: Let not this evil one, death, grasp me. If someone undertakes this vow, let him finish it to the end, whereby he will gain union with and residence with this divinity, breath.[92]

Here ends the fifth *Brāhmaṇa* of the first *Adhyāya*

Sixth *Brāhmaṇa*

The World as Name, Form and Action

1. This world is threefold: name, form and action. Amongst names, speech is the source,[93] because all names come from it. Speech is their common feature because it treats all names as equal. Speech is their foundation[94] because it supports all names.

2. Amongst form, sight is the source, because all forms come from it. Sight is their common feature because it treats all forms as equal. Sight is their foundation because it supports all forms.

3. Amongst actions, the body is the source, because all actions come from it. The body is their common feature because it treats all actions as equal. The body is their foundation because it supports all actions.

Although what is Real,[95] namely this physical world, is threefold, it is one: It is the *ātmā*. And although the *ātmā* is one, it is threefold:[96] It is the immortal covered by the Real. In this world, the immortal manifests as breath, while the Real manifests as name and form. Breath is always covered by these two.

Here ends the sixth *Brāhmaṇa* of the first *Adhyāya*
Here ends the first *Adhyāya*

---

[96] These last two sentences, *tad etat trayaṃ sad ekam ayam ātmā* and *atmo ekaḥ sann etat trayam,* may be read as a commentary on the famous Rig Veda verse (1.164.46) *ekaṃ sat viprā bahudhā vadanti* if *trayam* (threefold) is read as *bahudhā* (many). The big question arises how the word *sat* is to be understood. If read from the perspective of the later tradition, it would be God. If it is read from this early Upanishadic tradition, it would be this real threefold world.

Second *Adhyāya*

First *Brāhmaṇa*

Talks Between a Priest and a King

1. Once there was a priest, Balaki Garga by name. He spoke to the King of Kashi, Ajatashatru, and said, "Let me tell you about *brahma*."

King Ajatashatru replied, "For such a speech I will give you a thousand cows! People will run here saying, 'Janaka, Janaka, another Janaka is among us!'"[1]

2. So Balaki began, "That person you see in the sun I venerate as *brahma*."[2]

The king replied, "Don't speak to me about the sun. I salute him as preeminent, but only as the king and head of all beings. Indeed, a person who venerates him as such will himself become preeminent as a king and a head of all beings."

---

[1] Janaka is famous for being a wise and charitable king. See BU 1.4.

[2] What follows is a list of what might be obtained by the worship of *brahma* in this or that form. An extension of this thinking appears in later phases of the tradition, where the worship of a particular god will result in a particular benefit. For example, the worship of Prajapati will give good progeny. the worship of Durga will give power, the worship of the Vasus will result in wealth, etc. See Bhag. 2.3.2-7 for a list of what god or goddess will lead to what reward.

3. The priest continued, "That person we see in the moon I venerate as *brahma.*"

The king replied, "Don't speak to me about the moon. I salute him only as Soma, a king dressed in white. Indeed, a person who venerates him as such will have soma extract pressed every day and will have abundant food."[3]

4. The priest continued, "That person we see in lightning I venerate as *brahma.*"

The king replied, "Don't speak to me about lightning. I salute him only as a radiant one. A person who venerates him as such will himself become radiant, with strong and glorious offspring."

5. The priest continued, "That person we see in space[4] I venerate as *brahma.*"

The king replied, "Don't speak to me about space. I salute him only as immovable and complete. A person who venerates him as such will himself become replete with offspring and livestock. Indeed, his children will not depart this world prematurely."

---

[3] Moonlight was thought to have a favorable effect on the growth of vegetables and plants in general.

[4] Here the word is *ākāśa,* which does not refer only to outer space, but space in general, such as the distance between objects.

6. The priest continued, "That person we see in the wind I venerate as *brahma*."

The king replied, "Don't speak to me about wind. I salute him only as the invincible Indra with unconquerable armies. A person who venerates him as such will himself become invincible and triumphant over his enemies."

7. The priest continued, "That person we see in fire I venerate as *brahma*."

The king replied, "Don't speak to me about fire. I salute him only as victorious. A person who venerates him as such will also have victorious offspring."

8. The priest continued, "That person we see in water I venerate as *brahma*."

The king replied, "Don't speak to me about water. I salute him only as someone to be emulated. A person who venerates him as such will himself become emulated along with his descedants."

9. The priest continued, "That person we see in the mirror I venerate as *brahma*."

The king replied, "Don't speak to me about a reflection. I salute him only as a shining one. A person who venerates him as such will himself shine and his offspring will become glorious."

10. The priest continued, "That sound which follows a person after he passes by I venerate as *brahma*."

The king replied, "Don't speak to me about the sound of a passing person. I salute him only as life. Indeed, a person who venerates him as such will have a full life. His breath will not leave him before his apportioned time."

11. The priest continued, "That person we see in the directions I venerate as *brahma*."

The king replied, "Don't speak to me about the directions. I salute them only as fixed companions. A person who venerates them as such will always have companions and will never be separated from their clan."

12. The priest continued, "That person we see as a shadow I venerate as *brahma*."

The king replied, "Don't speak to me about a shadow. I salute him only as death. A person who venerates him as such will have a full life and death will not approach him before the proper time."

---

[5] This reversal of tradition is called *pratiloma*. The conventional way is called *anuloma*. *Loma* is hair, so, literally, *pratiloma* means against the hair, whereas *anuloma* is in the direction of the hair. This simply means going with the grain or against the grain. A king does not instruct a *brāhmana*. This is against the way of things; therefore, it is called *pratiloma*.

13. The priest continued, "That person we see in the body I venerate as *brahma*."

The king replied, "Don't speak to me about the body. I salute him only as one possessing a body. A person who venerates him as such will come to possess a body and his offspring will also possess a body."

With this the priest Balaki became silent.

14. King Ajatashatru asked, "Is that it?"

"That's it," replied Balaki.

"With just this *brahma* cannot be known," said the king.

Balaki Garga requested, "Then let me come to you as a student."

15. King Ajatashatru replied, "This is a reversal of tradition![5] When does a priest approach a king to know *brahma*? Nevertheless, I will teach you."

So King Ajatashatru took Balaki by the hand and the two of them went to a sleeping man. Speaking to this man by name, the king said, "Great King Soma of white robes, arise." But he did not get up. Finally, Ajatashatru touched him with his hand and woke him. He got up.

16. King Ajatashatru inquired, "As this man was sleeping, where was the person made of consciousness? And when he

awoke, from where did the person made of consciousness return?"

Balaki did not know.

---

[6] The word here is *prāṇa*. See fn to BU 1.3.7.

[7] Here the reference is obscure, but it is said that there are 72,000 "veins" around the heart area of the physical body that connect to the *purītat*. The dictionaries list *purītat* as the pericardium. Some commentators suggest, however, that the *purītat* is not a part of the physical body, but instead is the corresponding heart area of the subtle body and that, at the time of deep sleep, the consciousness moves from the physical body to the subtle body and rests at the *purītat* area of the subtle body. There are other references to this. See BU 4.2.3 and 4.3.20, CU 8.6.1 and MU 1.2.11.

[8] Some translators render this as the "height of sexual pleasure."

[9] Here again the word is *prāṇa*.

[10] *Asmāt ātmanah.* Literally, from one's *ātmā*.

[11] Here the expression is *prānā vai satyam, tesām esa satyam,* which means that the organs of the body and, by extension, this world, is *sat*, real. Yet behind this real is another Real, which is the *ātmā*. This is further evidence that at this stage of religious development the world was taken as *sat*, which is to say real, and not *asat,* unreal or illusory. See BU 1.6.3 and 2.3.1 for similar usages of the word *sat*.

17. King Ajatashatru stated, "While this man lay sleeping, the conscious person within takes his consciousness along with the power of his vital organs to rest at the space within his inner heart. When consciousness has been taken, then we say he is asleep. Thus breath is restrained, speech is restrained, the eye is restrained, the ear is restrained, and the mind is restrained.

18. "Wherever one goes during sleep, those places become his worlds. One becomes a 'great king' or a 'great priest' as it were. One goes high or one goes low, and as a king travels at will throughout his realm with his followers, so this one travels at will throughout his body along with the vital organs.[6]

19. "There are 72,000 pathways, called *hitās,* that lead from the heart to the *purītat.*[7] When one falls into deep sleep and loses all awareness, one slides through these pathways and rests at the *purītat*. There he rests, oblivious to everything, just as a young man, a great king or priest might rest oblivious to everything at the height of bliss.[8]

20. "As a spider sends forth its web from itself, as tiny sparks burst out from a fire, so all the vital organs,[9] all the worlds, all the gods and all beings spring forth from one's self.[10] This is the supreme mystery, the Real in the real: The vital functions are real, yet the *ātmā* is the Real behind this real."[11]

Here ends the first *Brāhmana* of the second *Adhyāya*

Second *Brāhmaṇa*

The Metaphor of the Body

1. There is a child who possesses a pot, a lid, a stick, and a rope.[12] One who knows this is able to control the seven envious relatives.[13] Indeed, this child is the main breath. The pot is its body, the lid its head, the stick its strength, and the rope its food.[14]

---

[12] This chapter is open to multiple interpretations. From one perspective it refers to the body, and from another perspective it refers to the celestial body. Implied is the relationship between the macrocosm and the microcosm, which is a common Vedic theme.

[13] The seven envious relatives are the two eyes, the two ears, the two nostrils, and the mouth. They are said to be envious because they pull the soul outward toward the physical world, by which it becomes attached to this world.

[14] Some say the child is the soul, others the subtle (astral) body, and still others the sun. The middle breath is the solar plexus, where the subtle body connects to the physical body. The container is the body or the universe. The lid is the head or the dome of the sky. The post is the breath or the spinal column, or the pole star. And the rope is the umbilical cord, or the silver cord that connects the subtle body with the physical body, or the Milky Way depending on the interpretation.

[15] Some take this as a reference to the Seven Sages within Ursa Major, the Big Dipper.

[16] Literally, his food supply never diminishes.

[17] Again, this is a reference to the Seven Sages within Ursa Major, the Big Dipper.

[18] Here the word is *prāṇa,* literally breath, but it can also refer to the senses, which are contained within the head. See fn to BU 1.3.7.

2. Seven imperishable things[15] always stand alongside this child. The first is the red streaks in the eye, by which the fierce Rudra is connected to him. Next there are the tears in the eyes, by which the rains are connected. Then there is the pupil of the eye, by which the sun is connected. Then there is the iris, by which fire is connected; the whites of the eye, by which Indra is connected; the lower eyelashes, by which the earth is connected; and, finally, the upper eyelashes, by which the sky is connected. One who understands becomes wealthy.[16]

3. In this regard there is the following verse:

There is a sacrificial vessel with its mouth turned down and its bottom facing up. Everything glorious is found within. Along its rim are the Seven Sages,[17] along with the eighth sage, speech, who can connect with *brahma*.

"A sacrificial vessel with its mouth turned down and its bottom facing up" is the head, because a head is like a vessel open at the bottom and closed at the top.

"Everything glorious is found within" refers to the vital functions.[18]

"On its rim are the Seven Sages," these too are the vital functions.

"And then there is speech, the eighth sage, who can connect with *brahma,*" for it is through speech that one may know *brahma*.

[19] In BU 4.2 2-3 the right and left eye are said to be Indha and Viraj, a husband and wife pair.

[20] The list of names of the seven stars within Ursa Major varies, but this is often one of the lists.

[21] There is a similar reference in BU 4.2.2 between Indha and Indra. There it is mentioned that the gods prefer the indirect to the direct. *Atti* then would be the indirect reference and *atri* the direct reference.

[22] To become an eater of the whole world means one becomes a consumer and enjoyer of all things. It is a common metaphor throughout the Upanishads.

[23] Here the word is *sat,* which refers to what is real, tangible and true. In the Hinduism of the Bhagavad Gita this refers to God and the soul. See BG 2.16. The opposite to *sat* is *asat,* which is the body and the physical world, because they are impermanent and therefore "unreal." But here, in this earlier Upanishadic Hinduism, *sat* refers to this tangible and concrete world that we see before us. This is just the opposite of how the word is used in the Gita and thus suggests a very different religious perspective. The usage as seen here first occurs in BU 1.6.3.

[24] The word here is *tya*, which is a neuter pronoun derived from *ta*, "that." In Sanskrit there is more than one kind of "that." Different pronouns are used to distinguish the "that" which is close from the "that" which is distant. In English the "that" which is close is generally indicated by the pronoun "this," whereas the "this" over there could be called "that." In Sanskrit the word for the "that" which is "over there" is *tya;* hence the translation "yonder there." So there are two forms of *brahma*, the real and tangible (*sat*), namely this physical *brahma* that we see before us, and the unseen and intangible "yonder" (*tya*) *brahma,* "out there." Together they form the whole of reality.

[25] In other words, it is this world.

[26] The verb here is *tapati*, from *tap,* to heat. The implication is that this formed aspect of *brahma* is compared to (continued page 53)

4. The two sages, Gottama and Bharadvaja, are the right ear and the left ear respectively. The two sages, Vishvamritra and Jamadagni, are the right eye and the left eye.[19] Vasishtha and Kashyapa are the right nostril and the left nostril. The sage Atri is speech.[20] Through speech one eats. Indeed, eating (*atti*) is the same as the word *atri*.[21] One who knows this becomes an eater of the world. Everything becomes his food.[22]

Here ends the second *Brāhmaṇa* of the second *Adhyāya*

Third *Brāhmaṇa*

Two Forms of *Brahma*

1. Indeed, there are two forms of *brahma*: one with form and the other without form, one mortal and the other immortal, one stationary and the other movable, one Real[23] and the other yonder there.[24]

2. The one with form is different from the wind and the sky. It is mortal. It is fixed. It is tangible.[25] The essence of this one with form, which is mortal, fixed and tangible, is heat, for heat is the essence of this tangible one.[26]

3. Now the other, without form, is like the wind and sky. It is immortal and movable. It is "that one," yonder. The one which is formless, immortal and movable is like the person within the orb of the sun. This is the essence of this one.

All this is in reference to the divinities.

the sun, while the other unformed aspect of *brahma* is compared to the unseen person within the sun. See the following verse.

[27] This Upanishad contains many eye references. The implication is that the eye is the path to the soul and to *brahma.* For other eye references see BU 2.2.2, 2.3.5, 2.3.6, 4.2.2, 5.5.2.

[28] The word is *indra-gopa*, which I have loosely translated as a firefly, but may in fact be some other small insect.

[29] See Kena Upanishad 4.4: *tasyaiṣa ādesah/ yad etad vidyuto vyadyutad ā3 itonnayamomiṣad ā3 ity adhidaivatam,* "Here is a teaching: The flash of lightning that causes one to blink and say, 'Ah!' – that experience of 'Ah', is Divinity." (The "ā3" seen in the transliteration is the "Ah." The "3" means the sound is held for three beats. This is called prolation and it is a feature of Vedic Sanskrit.)

[30] Here the word is *ādeśa*, which is generally translated as a "teaching." But the word is also used in the sense of "substitution," especially in grammar. *Brahma* is beyond description and so theologians often "substitute" other means to describe the indescribable. These other means include metaphor and indication by negation (see *apoha* in fn 31). It seems possible that *ādeśa* may also have this sense as well. For a similar usage see CU 3.5.1.

[31] This is the first usage of the famous *neti, neti—not this, not this—* expression. This is called *apoha*, indication by negation. One can describe a cow directly by saying such things as a cow is black and white, has horns, has four hooves and a tail, and so on. But one could also describe a cow indirectly, through exclusion, by saying it is not a horse, it is not a dog, it is not a cat, and so on until everything has been excluded except a cow. This is *apoha.* So "not this, not this" is an indirect way to describe *brahma.* Sometimes, when describing something intangible, the indirect method is the only way. For another usage of *neti neti* see BU 3.9.26. This is called apophatic theology within the Christian sphere, as opposed to cataphatic theology.

4. Now in reference to the body.

This *brahma* with form, which is different from the breath and the space within the body, which is mortal and immovable, this is the real *brahma.* The eye[27] is the essence of this *brahma* that is made of form and which is mortal and immovable. This is the essence of the real *brahma (sat).*

5. The formless *brahma,* on the other hand, is the same as breath and the space within the body. It is immortal and movable and it is this yonder *brahma*. The person within the right eye is the essence of this yonder *brahma,* who is formless, immortal and immovable.

6. The visible form of this person within the eye is like a golden garment, like fine white wool, a firefly,[28] a shooting flame, a white lotus, or a sudden flash of lightning.[29] And for one who knows this, his glory surges like a sudden flash of lightning.

So this is the teaching:[30] Not this! Not this![31] For beyond this "not" there is nothing higher! He is the Real of the real. Creatures who breathe and have vital functions are real, but he is the Real behind the real.

Here ends the third *Brāhmaṇa* of the second *Adhyāya*

[32] Yajnavalkya is a famous philosopher sage who appears throughout this Upanishad and the Shatapatha Brahmana. Here the word *sthanāt,* "from this place," is taken to mean from this state. Yajnavalkya is retiring from householder life and becoming renounced, *vānaprastha.* For a similar discussion see BU 4.5.

[33] His two wives are Maitreyi and Katyayani, and, as he quits the world, Yajnavalkya wants to settle his estate between his two wives. These two wives can be read as a metaphor. Each of us has two needs, our need for material satisfaction and our need for spiritual satisfaction.

[34] Here the word is *bhagavān,* a very special form of address usually reserved for gods, sages or saints.

[35] Here the word is *bata*, a term of deep affection. It shows the special relationship between Yajnavalkya and Maitreyi.

[36] The word repeatedly used in this section is *kāma*, which in the later language often refers to carnal pleasure. But here *kāma* simply means pleasure, happiness, love or joy, and we could use any of these words.

[37] Here the word is *ātmā,* a word that is open to a huge array of translation possibilities: God, the Self, *brahma*, the self, soul, spirit, breath, a reflexive pronoun, intellect, mind, understanding, essence, nature, and even the body, and more! So the meaning is contextual. How to translate and interpret this word is the great challenge for teachers and students of Hindu theology.

[38] This whole section suggests that all the things of this world provide opportunities to experience the soul; that the pleasures and joys one feels through relationships and things of this world actually arise from the pleasure and joy coming from the soul. Real pleasure and joy, therefore, come from spirit; and what we feel in this world as pleasure and joy are reflections of spiritual pleasure and joy.

Fourth *Brāhmaṇa*

The Joy of Soul

Conversation between a Husband and a Wife

1. Yajnavalkya declared, "My dear Maitreyi, as I am leaving this place,[32] I must make a final settlement between you and Katyayani."[33]

2. Maitreyi asked, "If I possessed all the wealth of this world, would it give me immortality?"

"No," replied Yajnavalkya. "It would only allow you to have a life of wealth. There is no hope of gaining immortality through wealth."

3. Maitreyi replied, "I have no use for what does not bring immortality. Please, exalted sir,[34] tell me what you know that can bring immortality."

4. Yajnavalkya said, "Ah,[35] Maitreyi, you have always been dear, and now you are speaking what is also dear to me. Come and sit, and I will explain it to you. While I speak, give me your full attention."

5. He began to speak. "A husband is dear not for the joy[36] a husband brings. Instead, a husband is dear for the joy of the *ātmā*[37] that a husband brings.[38] A wife is dear not for the joy a wife brings, but for the joy of the *ātmā* a wife brings. Sons are dear

not for the joys that sons bring, but for the joy of the *ātmā* that sons bring. Wealth is dear not for the joy that wealth brings, but for the joy of the *ātmā* that wealth brings. The priestly class is dear not for the joy the priestly class gives, but for the joy of the *ātmā* the priestly class gives. The warrior class is dear not for the joy the warrior class gives, but for the joy of the *ātmā* the warrior class gives. The worlds are dear not for the joy of the worlds, but for joy of the *ātmā* the worlds bring. The gods are dear not for the joy the gods give, but for joy of the *ātmā* the gods give. All beings are dear not for the joys all beings bring, but for the joy of the *ātmā* that all beings bring. One holds all things as dear not for the joy all things bring, but for joy of the *ātmā* all things bring.

"Oh Maitreyi, it is the *ātmā* alone that should be seen, heard, thought and reflected upon. For by seeing, hearing, thinking and reflecting upon the *ātmā* all things are known.

6. "The *brāhmaṇa* forsakes one who thinks a *brāhmaṇa* is different from the *ātmā*. The *kṣatriya* forsakes one who thinks a *kṣatriya* is different from the *ātmā*. The gods forsake one who thinks the gods are different from the *ātmā*. Beings forsake one who thinks beings are different from the *ātmā*. The universe forsakes one who thinks the universe is different from the *ātmā*. For the *brāhmaṇa, the kṣatriya,* the gods, all beings and the universe *are* the *ātmā*.

---

[39] The word is *vīṇā*.

[40] Here the full name of this Veda is *Atharva-āṅgirasa*.

[41] The word is *sankalpa*, which means imagining or conceptualizing.

7. "Consider this: When a drum is beaten one cannot grasp the outward sounds directly; only by taking hold of the drum itself or the drummer can one catch hold of the sounds.

8. "When a conch shell is blown one cannot grasp the outward sound directly; only by taking hold of the shell itself or the blower can one catch hold of the sound.

9. "When a stringed instrument[39] is played one cannot grasp the outward sounds directly; only by taking hold of the instrument itself or the player can one catch hold of the sounds.

10. "Or consider this: As smoke billows forth from a fire that has had wet fuel placed on it, so, my dear, from the outward breathing of that great being comes forth the Rig, Yajur, Sama, and Atharva[40] Vedas, the histories, the ancient stories, the sciences, the secret teachings, the verses, the aphorisms, the explanations and the commentaries. All these come from the breathing of this great being.

11. "As the ocean is the point of convergence for all waters, so the skin is the point of convergence for all touching. Similarly, the nose is the point of convergence for all fragrances, the tongue for all tastes, the eye for all form, the ear for all sounds, the mind for all thinking,[41] the heart for all sciences, the two hands for all actions, the sexual organ for all pleasures, the anus for all excretions, the two feet for all travels, and speech for all the Vedas.

12. "Again, consider this: When a lump of salt is thrown into water and dissolves, it is not possible to pick out any of the salt; yet everywhere it is salty. So this great being, infinite and without boundary, is a mass of perception everywhere. Arising from these elements it is also destroyed along with them. So I say after death there is no awareness." Thus spoke Yajnavalkya.

13. Maitreyi said, "Revered sir, when you say, after death there is no awareness, you confuse me."

Yajnavalkya replied, "My dear, I have said nothing confusing. What I have said is sufficient for understanding.

14. "In a situation where there is duality, as it were, one can smell another, one can see another, one can hear another, one can speak to another, and one can think of and perceive another. Yet when one's self has become all things,[42] by what means does one smell anything or anyone? Similarly, by what means does one see or hear or speak or think or perceive of anything or anyone? What is there to perceive and by what means? My dear, how can one even perceive the perceiver?"[43]

Here ends the fourth *Brāhmaṇa* of the second *Adhyāya*

---

[42] Which is to say when all of one's elements have gone back to the whole, i.e., when one has died.

[43] See BU 4.3 30-31 for a similar reference.

Fifth Brāhmaṇa

The Honey Teachings

1. The earth is honey to all beings and all beings are honey to the earth. The immortal and shining person who is in this earth, the immortal and shining person who is in this body, they are *ātmā.* It is immortal. It is *brahma.* It is all things.

2. Water is honey to all beings and all beings are honey to water. The immortal and shining person who is in water, the immortal and shining person who is in semen, they are *ātmā,* It is immortal. It is *brahma.* It is all things.

3. Fire is honey to all beings and all beings are honey to fire. The immortal and shining person who is in fire, the immortal and shining person who is in speech, they are *ātmā.* It is immortal. It is *brahma.* It is all things.

4. Wind is honey to all beings and all beings are honey to wind. The immortal and shining person who is in wind, the immortal and shining person who is in breath, they are *ātmā.* It is immortal. It is *brahma.* It is all things.

5. The sun is honey to all beings and all beings are honey to the sun. The immortal and shining person who is in this sun, the immortal and shining person who is in the eye, they are *ātmā.* It is immortal. It is *brahma.* It is all things.

6. The directions are honey to all beings and all beings are honey to the directions. The immortal and shining person who is in these directions, this immortal and shining person who is in the ear,[44] they are *ātmā.* It is immortal. It is *brahma.* It is all things.

7. The moon is honey to all beings and all beings are honey to the moon. The immortal and shining person who is in this moon, the immortal and shining person who is in the mind, they are *ātmā.* It is immortal. It is *brahma.* It is all things.

8. Lightning is honey to all beings and all beings are honey to lightning. The immortal and shining person who is in this flash of lightning, the immortal and shining person who exists in vigor, they are *ātmā.* It is immortal. It is *brahma.* It is all things.

9. Thunder is honey to all beings and all beings are honey to thunder. The immortal and shining person who is in thunder, the immortal and shining person who is in sound and tone, they are *ātmā.* It is immortal. It is *brahma.* It is all things.

10. Space is honey to all beings and all beings are honey to space. The immortal and shining person who exists in space,

---

[44] In the Upanishads the ear is always associated with the directions.

the immortal and shining person who is in the heart, they are *ātmā.* It is immortal. It is *brahma.* It is all things.

11. Dharma is honey to all beings and all beings are honey to dharma. The immortal and shining person who is in dharma, the immortal and shining person who is devoted to justice and virtue, they are *ātmā.* It is immortal. It is *brahma.* It is all things.

12. Truth is honey to all beings and all beings are honey to truth. The immortal and shining person who is in truth, the immortal and shining person who is devoted to truth, they are *ātmā.* It is immortal. It is *brahma.* It is all things.

13. Humanity is honey to all beings and all beings are honey to humanity. The immortal and shining person who is in humanity, the immortal and shining person who is human, they are *ātmā.* It is immortal. It is *brahma.* It is all things.

14. The soul is honey to all beings and all beings are honey to the soul. The immortal and shining person who is soul, the immortal and shining person who is in the body, they are *ātmā.* It is immortal. It is *brahma.* It is all things.

15. Truly this *ātmā* is the Lord and King of all beings. As spokes of a wheel are held together between the rim and the hub, so all beings, all gods, all worlds, all breath, and all bodies are tied to this *ātmā*.

16. These are the same Honey Teachings that Dadhyan, a sage

versed in the Atharva Veda, taught to the Ashvins.[45] Knowing this he declared:

'"As thunder signals rain I celebrate your awesome deed to know this knowledge. Through the head of a horse you have learned this honey doctrine."[46]

17. These are the same Honey Teachings that Dadhyan, a sage

---

[45] The following verses refer to a story cited in the Rig Veda which describes the sage Dadhyan, who received this secret Honey Doctrine from Indra with the warning that if he ever disclosed it to anyone, Indra would have his head. When the two Aśvin brothers asked the sage for these teachings, they devised a plan to thwart Indra's curse by replacing the sage's head with a horse's head. When Indra carried out his threat and took the horse's head from the sage, the two Ashvins gave the sage back his original head.

[46] See RV 1.116.12 and SB 14.1.1 and 4.

[47] See RV 1.117.22.

[48] The word is *puram*, which means a fort. The body is often compared to a fort. See BG 5.13.

[49] Here a bird is a metaphor for the subtle body, sometimes called the astral body.

[50] The word *indra* here means the *ātmā* who enters endless forms and appears as the individual soul.

[51] This number of horses refers to the endless physical forms this lord, the *ātmā,* may inhabit. As many bodies as there are, this Indra takes their forms. His chariots and horses are multiplied according to the forms in which he appears.

[52] The word is *hari* and it refers to Indra's horses. These are the senses.

[53] See RV 6.47.18.

versed in the Atharva Veda, taught to the Ashvins. Knowing this he declared:

"O Ashvins, you have placed a horse's head on Dadhyan, of Atharva lore, and to keep his promise he taught you Indra's honey doctrine, which is now your secret."[47]

18. These are the same Honey Teachings that Dadhyan, a sage versed in the Atharvam Veda, taught to the Ashvins. Knowing this he declared:

"He made bodies[48] with two feet; he made bodies with four feet. Becoming a bird,[49] this person has entered these bodies.

"This indeed is the person dwelling in all bodies. There is nothing that is not covered by this One, there is nothing that is concealed from this One."

19. These are the same Honey Teachings that Dadhyan, a sage versed in the Atharva Veda, taught to the Ashvins. Knowing this he declared:

"He became the likeness of each and every form. For being seen he takes these forms. Indra[50] moves about in all these forms through his magic. Ten times a hundred[51] his horses[52] are yoked.[53]

"He alone is the steed, the ten and the hundred. He alone is the many. He alone is boundless. Indeed, this *brahma* is without a before, without an after, without an inside, without an outside. This *brahma* is the *ātmā*. This *brahma* knows all things. This is the teaching!"

Here ends the fifth *Brāhmaṇa* of the second *Adhyāya*

Sixth *Brāhmaṇa*

The Lineage of Teachers and Students[54]

1. Now the lineage of teachers:
Pautimāṣya received this teaching from Gaupavana,
Gaupavana from Pautimāṣya,
Pautimāṣya from Gaupavana,
Gaupavana from Kauśika,
Kauśika from Kauṇḍinya,
Kauṇḍinya from Śāṇḍilya,
Śāṇḍilya from Kauśika and Gautama,
Gautama (2) from Āgniveśya,
Āgniveśya from Śāṇḍilya and Ānabhimlāta,
Ānabhimlāta from Ānabhimlāta,
Ānabhimlāta from Ānabhimlāta,
Ānabhimlāta from Gautama,
Gautama from Saitava and Prācīnayogya,
Saitava and Prācīnayogya from Pārāśarya,
Pārāśarya from Bhāradvāja,

---

54. There are two other teacher/student lineage lists in this Upanishad. See BU 4.6 and 6.5. These kinds of lists are called *paramparas* and they are meant to show the authenticity of the teachings. Such lists always begin with God or, in this case, *brahma* (at the end of the list).

Bhāradvāja from Bhāradvāja and Gautama,
Gautama from Bhāradvāja,
Bhāradvāja from Pārāśarya,
Pārāśarya from Vaijavāpāyana,
Vaijavāpāyana from Kauśikāyani,
Kauśikāyanī (3) from Ghṛtakauśika,
Ghṛtakauśika from Pārāśaryāyaṇa,
Pārāśaryāyaṇa from Pārāśarya,
Pārāśarya from Jātūkarṇya,
Jātūkarṇya from Āsurāyana and Yāska,
Āsurāyana from Traivaṇi,
Traivaṇi from Aupajandhani,
Aupajandhani from Āsuri,
Āsuri from Bhāradvāja,
Bhāradvāja from Ātreya,
Ātreya from Māṇṭi,
Māṇṭi from Gautama,
Gautama from Gautama,
Gautama from Vātsya,
Vātsya from Śāṇḍilya,
Śāṇḍilya from Kaiśorya Kāpya,
Kaiśorya Kāpya from Kumārahārita,
Kumārahārita from Gālava,
Gālava from Vidarbhīkauṇḍinya,
Vidarbhīkauṇḍinya from Vatsanapād Bābhrava,
Vatsanapād Bābhrava from Panthāḥ Saubhara,
Panthāḥ Saubhara from Ayāsya Āṅgirasa,
Ayāsya Āṅgirasa from Ābhūti Tvāṣṭra,
Ābhūti Tvāṣṭra from Viśvarūpa Tvāṣṭra,
Viśvarūpa Tvāṣṭra from the two Ashvins,

the two Ashvins from Dadhyañc Ātharvaṇa,
Dadhyañc Ātharvaṇa from Atharvan Daiva,
Atharvan Daiva from Mṛtyu Prādhvaṃsana,
Mṛtyu Prādhvaṃsana from Prādhvaṃsana,
Prādhvaṃsana from Ekaṛṣi,
Ekaṛṣi from Vipracitti,
Vipracitti from Vyaṣṭi,
Vyaṣṭi from Sanāru,
Sanāru from Sanātana,
Sanātana from Sanaga,
Sanaga from Parameṣṭin,
Parameṣṭin from *brahma.*[55]
Brahma is the Self-existent. Adoration to *brahma*!

Here ends the sixth *Brāhmaṇa* of the second *Adhyāya*
Here ends the second *Adhyāya*

55. Some commentators interpret this *brahma* as the creator god Brahmā. See fn under BU 1.3.21.

Third *Adhyāya*

First *Brāhmaṇa*

The King's Challenge
Conversations with Yajnavalkya

1. King Janaka of Videha arranged a sacrifice with lavish gifts for his priests. From far and wide, priests from Kuru and Panchala assembled. King Janaka wanted to know which priest was the most learned, so he corralled a thousand cows and tied ten gold coins to each of their horns as a prize.

2. He addressed the learned assembly, "Most honorable sirs, let the most learned of you take these cows!"

But none among them dared.

Finally Yajnavalkya spoke to his disciple, "Samashrava, my son, take them!" He did.

The remaining priests became enraged and declared, "How dare he think he is the best amongst us!"

Now, King Janaka had a chief priest,[1] Ashvala by name, who asked Yajnavalkya, "Do you really think you are the best among us?"

---

[1] Here the word is *hotri*. In a sacrifice there are four main priests: the *hotri*, the *adhvaryu*, the *udgātri,* and the *brahma.*

Yajnavalkya replied, "For sure I bow to the most learned priest, but in truth I just wanted the cows!"

Thereupon, the chief priest Ashvala began to question him.

3. "Yajnavalkya, given that this whole world is in the grip of death—that all things are overcome by death—how can the patron of a sacrifice free himself from this grip?"

Yajnavalkya replied, "The patron of a sacrifice can free himself by means of the *hotri* priest,[2] the fire, and speech. Indeed, the *hotri* is the speech of the sacrifice. Therefore, speech, fire, and the *hotri* all lead to liberation."

4. "Yajnavalkya," Ashvala continued, "given that this whole world is in the grip of day and night—that all things are overcome by day and night[3]—how can the patron of a sacrifice free himself from this grip?"

---

[2] The *hotri* priest was the chief priest and the one expert in reciting the Rig Veda. He was the main chanter during a sacrifice.

[3] This is to say, time.

[4] The *adhvaryu* priest is expert in the Yajur Veda. He performs the practical work of arranging a sacrifice, which includes measuring everything out, building the altar, preparing sacrificial vessels, supplying wood, water and ghee, lighting the fire, bringing the animal and so forth.

[5] The *udgātri* priest is expert in singing the Sama Veda.

[6] The *brahma* priest is proficient in the Atharva Veda and would act as the "observing" priest to catch errors in recitation or procedure.

Yajnavalkya replied, "By means of the *adhvaryu* priest,[4] by means of the eye, and by means of the sun. Indeed, the *adhvaryu* priest is the eye of the sacrifice. Therefore, the eye, this yonder sun, and the *adhvaryu* priest all lead to liberation."

5. "Yajnavalkya, given that this whole world is in the grip of the waxing and waning moon—that all things are overcome by this waxing and waning—how can the patron of a sacrifice free himself from this grip?"

Yajnavalkya replied, "By means of the *udgātri* priest,[5] by means of the wind, and by means of breath. Indeed, the *udgātri* is the breath of the sacrifice. Therefore, breath, wind, and the *udgātri* priest all lead to liberation."

6. "Yajnavalkya, given that the sky is without support, how does the patron of a sacrifice reach heaven without a step?"

Yajnavalkya replied, "By means of the *brahma* priest,[6] by means of the mind, by means of the moon. Indeed, the *brahma* priest is the mind of the sacrifice. Therefore, this mind, this yonder moon, this *brahma* priest, all lead to liberation. All this is complete liberation. Now the treasure, please."

"Not so fast!" replied Ashvala.

7. Ashvala again inquired, "Yajnavalkya, during today's sacrifice, how many kinds of Rig verses will the *hotri* priest employ?"

"Three."

"What are these three?" asked Ashvala.

"The invocation verses, the verses accompanying the sacrifice itself, and the concluding verses of praise."[7]

"What comes as a result of these three?" asked Ashvala.

"Indeed, there is benefit to all beings who have breath!"

8. "Yajnavalkya, during today's sacrifice, how many kinds of oblations will the *adhvaryu* priest offer?"

---

[7] The *anuvākyā,* the *yājyā* and the *śasyā* are three types of mantras recited by the *hotri* priest, at the commencement of the sacrifice, during the sacrifice, and at the conclusion.

[8] The first oblations are comprised of wood and ghee, the second of flesh, and the third of milk and *soma* juice. Ghee makes the flame flare up, meat makes the fire spread out, and milk and *soma* juice cause the fire to go down. Some commentators take the second oblation (*atinedante*) as causing the fire to sizzle.

[9] *Deva-loka*, the world of the gods.

[10] *Pitṛ-loka*, the world of the forefathers.

[11] *Manuṣya-loka*, the world of men.

[12] Here the word is *manas*, which is usually rendered as mind or cognitive function. But the real power of the mind is its ability to imagine all things.

[13] In the Rig Veda the word *viśva-deva* refers to all of the gods, but in the later Vedas it refers to a specific class of deities sometimes enumerated as nine or twelve specific deities.

"Three."

"So what are these three?" asked Ashvala.

Yajnavalkya answered, "The oblations that cause the fire to flame up, the oblations that cause the fire to spread out, and the oblations that suppress the fire."[8]

"What does one gain as a result?" asked Ashvala.

"One gains the world of the gods[9] by the oblations that flame the fire up because the world of the gods shines like fire. One gains the world of the ancestors[10] by the oblations that spread out and sizzle because the world of the ancestors is spread all around as it were. One gains the world of men[11] by the oblations that suppress the fire because the world of men is seemingly down," replied Yajnavalkya.

9. Ashvala continued, "O Yajnavalkya, during today's sacrifice, how many divinities will the *brahma* priest, who sits on the southern side, evoke to protect the fire?"

"Just one."

"And who is that one?" asked Ashvala.

"Imagination.[12] Indeed, imagination is boundless, so all these divinities[13] are boundless. And because imagination is boundless, he conquers this world."

10. "Yajnavalkya, during today's sacrifice, how many hymns will the *udgātri* priest sing?" asked Ashvala.

"Three."

"What are these three?" asked Ashvala.

---

[14] The three breaths mentioned here are *prāṇa*, *apāna* and *vyāna*, namely the in-breath, the out-breath and the held-breath. Through the in-breath energy is brought into the body, through the out-breath waste products are eliminated, and through the in-between or held-breath energy is diffused throughout the body. Sometimes two other breaths are mentioned, namely *uḍāna* and *samāna*, which have to do with digestion and sounding. For more information on these three breaths see CU 1.3.

[15] Here the words respectively are *pṛthivī-loka*, *antarikṣa-loka*, and *dyu-loka*. This is akin to the three utterances, *bhūr*, *bhuvas* and *svas*, the low, the middle and the high regions, used in the recitation of *gāyatrī* and other mantras.

[16] Here the words are *graha* and *atigraha*. Both come from the root *grah*, which means to grasp. Literally, *graha* means "to seize" or "to take hold of." In fact, the English word "grab" is cognate with *graha*. So that which "grabs or takes hold of" is a *graha*. *Ati-graha* is literally an "over-grabber." So the *ati-grahas* grab the *grahas*. In the following verses these *grahas* and their *atigrahas* will be enumerated. In this section the *grahas* are the senses and the *atigrahas* are the object of the senses. In the language of the BG, there is a similar enumeration between the senses and their objects, only there the language is *indriya* and *indriya-artha,* which is more literal. There it is also interesting that the grabbing is in the reverse order, the senses grab the sense objects. Here the order is reversed, the sense objects grab the senses.

"The invocation verses, the verses accompanying the sacrifice, and the concluding verses of praise."

"In reference to the body, what is the meaning of these verses?" asked Ashvala.

"The invocation verses are the incoming breath,[14] the verses accompanying the sacrifice are the outgoing breath, and the concluding verses of praise are the in-between breath."

"And what does one gain as a result?" asked Ashvala.

"Through the invocation verses one gains the earthly worlds, through the accompanying verses one gains the atmosphere worlds, and through the concluding verses one gains the heavenly worlds,"[15] replied Yajnavalkya.

Thereafter the *hotri* priest Ashvala ceased questioning.

Here ends the first *Brāhmaṇa* of the third *Adhyāya*

Second *Brāhmaṇa*

The Senses and Their Objects

1. Next Jaratkarava Artabhaga began to question, "Yajnavalkya, how many senses are there and how many objects of the senses are there?"[16]

"There are eight senses and eight objects of the senses," replied Yajnavalkya.

"So what are these eight senses and what are the eight objects of these senses?"

2. "The nose[17] is a sense organ which is ruled by the outgoing breath, and thereby odor is apprehended by the outgoing breath.[18]

3. "Speech is a sense organ which is ruled by name, and thereby name is articulated by speech.

4. "The tongue is a sense organ which is ruled by taste, and thereby taste is apprehended by the tongue.

5. "The eye is a sense organ which is ruled by form, and thereby form is seen by the eye.

6. "The ear is a sense organ which is ruled by sound, and thereby sound is heard by the ear.

7. "The mind is a sense organ which is ruled by desire, and

---

[17] Here the word is *prāṇa*, which generally means breath. However, *prāṇa* also means "life force" and even "sense organ." Here it is translated as "nose." This is a gloss of course, yet it can be justified by context. In this regard there is an expression, *prāṇa-randhra*, meaning "breath opening" to indicate the nose or mouth.

[18] The idea is that in-breath and out-breath are related to each other as sense organ and sense object, which results in the ability to experience odor.

thereby desire is controlled by the mind.

8. "The hands are a sense organ which are ruled by action, and thereby action is performed by the hands.

9. "The skin is a sense organ which is ruled by touch, and thereby touch is apprehended by the skin.

"These are the eight sense organs along with their eight objects," replied Yajnavalkya.

10. Artabhaga continued, "Yajnavalkya, since we know this whole world is food for death, who is that god for whom death is food?"

"Indeed, fire is death, yet death is food for water. Knowing this, a person overcomes repeated death," replied Yajnavalkya.

11. "Yajnavalkya, when a person dies, do the life airs leave or not?"

"No," replied Yajnavalkya, "they collect and swell, causing the body to bloat. So a dead person lays bloated."

12. "Yajnavalkya, when a person dies, what is it that does not leave?"

"His name, for name is eternal like all these gods. One who understands this wins an eternal world!" replied Yajnavalkya.

13. "Yajnavalkya, when a person dies, when his speech merges with fire, when his breath goes to the wind, when his sight goes to the sun, when his mind merges with the moon, when his hearing goes to the directions, when his physical body goes to the earth, when his self goes to the ether, when his bodily hair goes to the plants and the hair on his head goes to the trees, when his blood and semen are absorbed by waters, what in fact becomes of this person?"

Yajnavalkya replied, "My dear Artabhaga, take my hand. Only the two of us should know of this. This should remain between the two of us."

Both of them departed and conferred. Of what did they speak? They spoke of action. What did they praise? They praised action. One becomes good through good deeds; one becomes evil by bad deeds. Thereafter Jaratkarava Artabhaga remained silent.

Here ends the second *Brāhmana* of the third *Adhyāya*

---

[19] A Gandharva is an astral spirit.

[20] No doubt this section is obscure. The distance the sun travels in thirty-two days suggests a 30-degree segment of the solar ecliptic, a sign of the zodiac. "Surrounding it, covering twice the distance, is the size of the earth" suggests the region of the sun's path below the horizon. This also suggests knowledge that the earth is a globe and not flat.

[21] This is the place where the ocean and the sky meet, i.e., the horizon.

Third *Brāhmaṇa*

Where Performers of the Horse Sacrifice Go

1. Next Bhujya Lahyayani questioned, "Yajnavalkya, once, traveling through the Madras region, I came to the house of Pancala Kapya. There I met his daughter, who was possessed by a Gandharva.[19] So I asked that spirit who he was, and he replied that he was Sudhanva Angirasa. In the course of discussing various things, I asked this Gandharva, 'Where are the descendants of the Parikshitas?' So I ask the same of you, Yajnavalkya, where are the descendants of the Parikshitas?"

2. Yajnavalkya relied, "That Gandharva no doubt told you they have gone to the place where those who perform the horse sacrifice go."

"So where do those who perform horse sacrifices go?"

Yajnavalkya answered, "The distance the sun's chariot travels in thirty-two days is the size of this visible world. Surrounding it, covering twice the distance, is the size of the earth,[20] and around it, covering twice that distance again, is the ocean. Now, there is a space between the two[21] as thin as a razor's edge or a mosquito's wing. Indra, assuming the form of a magical bird, handed the Pārikṣitas to the wind. The wind then placed them within himself and carried them to the performers of the horse sacrifice. In this way that Gandharva praised the wind. Therefore, the wind is both the individual and the aggregate.[22] One who understands this avoids repeated death."

Thereupon Bhujya Lahyayani remained silent.

Here ends the third *Brāhmana* of the third *Adhyāya*

Fourth *Brāhmaṇa*

The *Ātmā* within All

1. Then Ushasta Cakrayaṇa began to question. "Yajnavalkya, please tell me about that *brahma* who is directly perceivable and not hidden, and who is the *ātmā*[23] within all."

"This *ātmā* within all is your *ātmā*."

"But, Yajnavalkya, who is that *ātmā* within all?"

---

[22] Here the words *vyaṣṭi* and *samaṣṭi* refer to the part and the whole, the particular and the universal.

[23] On the use of the word *ātmā,* see fn under BU 1.2.1.

[24] *Prāṇa* is the in-breath. See fn to BU 1.3.7 and CU 1.3.3.

[25] *Apāṇa* is the out-breath. *Ibid.*

[26] *Vyāna* is the breath that is held between breathing in and breathing out. See CU 1.3.3.

[27] *Udāna,* the up-breath.

[28] Here the word is *vijñātṛ*, which can also be translated as "knower" or "the one who understands."

"The one who breathes with the in-breath,[24] that one is your *ātmā* and the *ātmā* of all. The one who breathes with the out-breath,[25] that one is your *ātmā* and the *ātmā* of all. The one who breathes with the in-between breath,[26] that one is your *ātmā* and the *ātmā* of all. The one who breathes with the sounding-breath,[27] that one is your *ātmā* and the *ātmā* of all. These breaths are your *ātmā* and the *ātmā* within all."

2. Ushasta Cakrayaṇa continued, "This is like saying 'This is a cow, this is a horse.' You've not really told me anything. Please tell me about that *brahma* who is directly perceivable and not hidden, and who is the *ātmā* within all."

"This *ātmā* within all is your *ātmā*."

"But, Yajnavalkya, who is that *ātmā* within all?"

"One cannot see the seer who does the seeing, one cannot hear the hearer who does the hearing, one cannot think of the thinker who does the thinking, and one cannot perceive the perceiver who does the perceiving.[28] That one is your *ātmā* and the *ātmā* of all. All else is suffering."

Thereupon Ushasta Cakrayaṇa remained silent.

Here ends the fourth *Brāhmana* of the third *Adhyāya*

Fifth *Brāhmaṇa*

The *Ātmā* within All

1. Then Kahola Kaushitakeya began to question, "Yajnavalkya, please tell me about that *brahma* who is directly perceivable

[29] Traditionally, the *brāhmana* is the first of the four *varṇas* in the Hindu social system and he makes his livelihood through study and teaching, performing rituals and giving counsel, etc. As a householder making his livelihood through learning, he is known as a pandit, a learned person. Before becoming a householder, as a student he was known as a *brahmacarya*. It is a simple life free of the encumbrances of the world. After living as a householder he again goes back to a more simple life and retires to the next stage, called *vanaprastha*, literally the "forest dweller." The final phase is to live as a monk, completely renouncing the world. To become as a child is to give up the worldly life and to live as a *brahmacarya* or *vanaprastha*. In other words, it means to live a simple life.

[30] Here the word is *muni*. In other words, it means to live as a *sannyāsī*, completely renounced.

[31] The literal meaning of *brāhmana* is "one in relation to *brahma*," i.e., a knower of *brahma*.

[32] Ultimately, being a *brāhmana* is a state of understanding and perception, i.e., being a knower of *brahma*, which has no bearing on whether one is a student, a householder, a forest dweller or a monk. Yet, to achieve that understanding one has to go through all stages of life, from simple to complex to renounced.

[33] Here the words *ota* and *prota* refer to the woven threads that make up fabric. This is warp and woof. The up and down threads are the warp, and the crossing threads are the woof. Another translation could be "back and forth," The metaphoric meaning is, of course, support.

and not hidden, and who is the *ātmā* within all."

"This *ātmā* within all is your *ātmā.*"

"But, Yajnavalkya, who is that *ātmā* within all?"

"It is the one who is completely untouched by hunger, thirst, grief, illusion, old age and death. *Brāhmanas* who have come to understand this *ātmā* within all resist the desire for sons, wealth and worlds, and seek the ways of asceticism. After all, the desire for sons leads to the desire for wealth, and the desire for wealth leads to the desire for worlds. Both of these are simply desires. Therefore, let the *brāhmana* give up being a pandit and become as a child.[29] When he has become disgusted with living as both a pandit and a child, he becomes a sage.[30] And when he has become tired of both the worldly life as well as the ascetic life, he becomes a real *brāhmana*.[31] In this way he remains a *brāhmana* no matter how he lives.[32] All else is suffering."

Thereupon Kahola Kaushitakeya remained silent.

Here ends the fifth *Brāhmaṇa* of the third *Adhyāya*

Sixth *Brāhmaṇa*

Gārgi Questions Yajnavalkya
The Support of the Worlds

1. Then Gargi Vacakvani began to question, "Yajnavalkya, since this whole world is woven warp and woof[33] on waters, on what

are waters woven, warp and woof?"

"On the wind, O Gargi," replied Yajnavalkya.

"On what is the wind woven, warp and woof?" asked Gargi.

"On the atmosphere worlds, O Gargi."

"On what are the atmosphere worlds woven, warp and woof?"

"On the worlds of the Gandharvas, O Gargi."

"On what are the worlds of the Gandharvas woven, warp and woof?"

"On the worlds of the Adityas,[34] O Gargi."

---

[34] The word *āditya* means "relating to the sun." There are twelve *ādityas* referring to the name of the sun in each sign of the zodiac.

[35] The word for lunar mansions is *nakṣtra*. There are twenty-seven *nakṣtras* corresponding to a segment of thirteen and one-third degrees of the solar ecliptic. This is the distance the moon travels in a day against the background of stars.

[36] The Prajapatis are the progenitors of creation, said to be ten in number.

[37] This could also be rendered as "on the worlds of Brahmā," meaning the creator god Brahmā. The Sanskrit reads *brahma-lokeṣu,* so "*brahma*" can be read as masculine or neuter. As masculine it becomes Brahmā, the creator god; as neuter it becomes *brahma*, the all-pervading "force."

"On what are the worlds of the Adityas woven, warp and woof?"

"On the worlds of the moon, O Gargi."

"On what are the worlds of the moon woven, warp and woof?"

"On the worlds of the lunar mansions,[35] O Gargi."

"On what are the worlds of the lunar mansions woven, warp and woof?"

"On the worlds of the gods, O Gargi."

"On what are the worlds of the gods woven, warp and woof?"

"On the worlds of Indra, O Gargi."

"On what are the worlds of Indra woven, warp and woof?"

"On the worlds of the Prajapatis,[36] O Gargi."

"On what are the worlds of the Prajapatis woven, warp and woof?"

"On the worlds of *brahma,*[37] O Gargi."

"On what are the worlds of *brahma* woven, warp and woof?"

Yajnavalkya spoke, "Gargi, do not over question lest your head shake apart. You ask too many questions concerning a divinity about whom too many questions cannot be asked. Therefore, ask no more."

Thereupon Gargi Vacakvani remained silent.

Here ends the sixth *Brāhmana* of the third *Adhyāya*

Seventh *Brāhmaṇa*
Uddalaka Questions Yajnavalkya
The Force Within

1. Then Uddalaka Aruni began to speak. "Yajnavalkya, once while we were studying ritual at the house of Patancala Kapya near Madras, we saw he had a wife possessed by a Gandharva spirit. We asked that spirit who he was, to which that spirit replied, 'I am Kabandha Atharvaṇa.' That Gandharva then asked Patancala Kapya and the other students of ritual, 'Kapya, do you

---

[38] Here the word is *antaryāmin,* which I have translated as "the force within." It may also be rendered as "the inner controller." The word is comprised of *antar-yam*. *Antar* means the inside of anything and *yam* means to control, hence the idea of inner controller.

[39] The word here is *vāyu,* which I have translated as "breath." It could also be translated as "wind" or "air." In the Upanishads and elsewhere, there is always a correlation between wind and breath. This is the relationship between the macrocosm and the microcosm. The air within is the wind without, and so on.

[40] *Antaryāmin*, see fn under 3/7/1.

know that thread by which this world and the world beyond and all these beings are woven together?' Patancala Kapya relied, 'My good sir, that I do not know.' The Gandharva spirit then asked Patancala Kapya and the other students, 'Kapya, do you know the force within[38] this world and world beyond and of all beings?' Patancala Kapya relied, 'My good sir, that I also do not know.' That spirit then told Patancala Kapya and the other students, 'One who knows this thread and this force within knows *brahma*, knows the worlds, knows the gods, knows the Vedas, knows all beings, knows the soul, and so knows all things.' And I know it! So, Yajnavalkya, if you drive away these *brahma*-cows without knowing that binding thread or that force within, your head will surely shake apart."

Yajnavalkya replied, "Gautama, indeed, I do know that thread and that force within!"

"Anyone can say, 'I know, I know,' but what do you really know?" questioned Uddalaka.

2. Yajnavalkya replied, "Breath[39] is that thread. By breath, O Gautama, this world, the world beyond and all beings are strung together. Therefore they say of a dead man 'His bodily parts have become slackened.' It is by the thread of breath that they are strung together."

"Indeed this is so, Yajnavalkya," declared Uddalaka. "Now tell us about the force within."[40]

3. Yajnavalkya declared, "That which exists within earth yet is different from earth, who is unknown to earth, whose body earth is and who controls from within, is the immortal force within. It is the *ātmā.*

4. "That which exists within waters yet is different from waters, who is unknown to waters, whose body water is and who controls from within, is the immortal force within. It is the *ātmā.*

5. "That which exists within fire yet is different from fire, who is unknown to fire, whose body fire is and who controls from within, is the immortal force within. It is the *ātmā.*

6. "That which exists within sky[41] yet is different from sky, who

---

[41] The word is *antarīkṣa,* and it refers to the intermediary space between earth and heaven. This word has a similar construction to *antaryāmin* except it is *antar-īkṣ.* The verbal root *īkṣ* means to see; thus, *antarīkṣa* refers to what is "seen within." The realm of the earth is the lower level. In much of Hinduism there is reference to three worlds: *bhūr, bhuvas* and *svar*. These worlds get interpreted in various ways, but the most basic interpretation is that *bhūr* is the terrestrial realm, *bhuvas* is the sky and atmosphere region where birds fly, for example, and *svar* is the region of space where the planets and stars exist. A*ntarīkṣa* is the in-between region, i.e., *bhūva,* the region between *bhūr* and *svar.*

[42] Here the word is *dyu,* and it is used in the sense of outer space or the place where the planets exist.

[43] Here the word is *ākāśa,* which is commonly translated as "space." Here space means the distance between any two points.

is unknown to sky, whose body sky is and who controls from within, is the immortal force within. It is the *ātmā*.

7. "That which exists within wind yet is different from wind, who is unknown to wind, whose body wind is and who controls from within, is the immortal force within. It is the *ātmā*.

8. "That which exists within the heavens[42] yet is different from the heavens, who is unknown to the heavens, whose body the heavens are and who controls from within, is the immortal force within. It is the *ātmā*.

9. "That which exists within the sun yet is different from the sun, who is unknown to the sun, whose body the sun is and who controls from within, is the immortal force within. It is the *ātmā*.

10. "That which exists within the directions yet is different from the directions, who is unknown to the directions, whose body the directions are and who controls from within, is the immortal force within. It is the *ātmā*.

11. "That which exists within the moon and stars yet is different from the moon and stars, who is unknown to the moon and stars, whose body the moon and stars are and who controls from within, is the immortal force within. It is the *ātmā*.

12. "That which exists within space[43] yet is different from space, who is unknown to space, whose body space is and who controls from within, is the immortal force within. It is the *ātmā*.

13. "That which exists within darkness yet is different from darkness, who is unknown to darkness, but whose body darkness is and who controls from within, is the immortal force within. It is the *ātmā*.

14. "That which exists within light yet is different from light, who is unknown to light, but whose body light is and who controls from within, is the immortal force within. It is the *ātmā*.

"All this is in reference to the divinities.[44]

15. "Now hear it in reference to beings.[45] That which exists within all beings yet is different from all beings, who is unknown to all beings, but whose body all beings are and who controls from within, is the immortal force within. It is the *ātmā*.

"That was in reference to beings.

16. "Now hear it in reference to the body.[46] That which exists within breath yet is different from breath, who is unknown to breath, but whose body breath is and who controls from within, is the immortal force within. It is the *ātmā*.

---

[44] The word here is *adhidaivata,* relating to the devas. The three terms used here, *adhidaivata, adhibhuta* and *adhyātmā,* are used in BG 8.1-4.

[45] Here the word is *adhibhūta*, relating to beings.

[46] Here the word is *adhyātmā,* where the word *ātmā* clearly means body. See also BU 5.14.4.

17. "That which exists within speech yet is different from speech, who is unknown to speech, but whose body speech is and who controls from within, is the immortal force within. It is the *ātmā*.

18. "That which exists within the eye yet is different from the eye, who is unknown to the eye, but whose body the eye is and who controls from within, is the immortal force within. It is the *ātmā*.

19. "That which exists within the ear yet is different from the ear, who is unknown to the ear, but whose body the ear is and who controls from within, is the immortal force within. It is the *ātmā*.

20. "That which exists within mind yet is different from mind, who is unknown to mind, but whose body mind is and who controls from within, is the immortal force within. It is the *ātmā*.

21. "That which exists within the skin yet is different from the skin, who is unknown to the skin, but whose body the skin is and who controls from within, is the immortal force within. It is the *ātmā*.

22. "That which exists within understanding yet is different from understanding, who is unknown to understanding, but whose body understanding is and who controls from within, is the immortal force within. It is the *ātmā*.

23. "That which exists within semen yet is different from semen, who is unknown to semen, but whose body semen is and who controls from within, is the immortal force within. It is the *ātmā*.

"This one is the unseen seer, the unheard hearer, the unthinkable thinker, the imperceivable perceiver. Other than this one, no one sees; other than this one, no one hears; other than this one, no one thinks; and other than this one, no one perceives. This one alone is the immortal force within. This one is your *ātmā*. Besides this all else is suffering."

Thereupon Uddalaka Aruni remained silent.

Here ends the seventh *Brāhmaṇa* of the third *Adhyāya*

Eighth *Brāhmaṇa*

Gargi Questions Yajnavalkya Once More

1. Gargi[47] again said, "Honorable gentlemen, I have two questions to ask Yajnavalkya. If he can answer these questions, I doubt any of you will be able to defeat him in this learned discussion of *brahma*."

---

[47] Here Gargi is addressed by her *gotra* name, Vacakvani. She has previously appeared in BU 3.6.

[48] The word is *ākāśa*, space, in the sense of the distance between two points.

"Ask, O Gargi," replied Yajnavalkya.

2. Gargi said, "Yajnavalkya, as a fierce son of Kashi strings his bow and loads it with two enemy-piercing arrows, I challenge you with these two questions. Answer these questions."

"Ask, O Gargi," replied Yajnavalkya.

3. Gargi asked, "Yajnavalkya, all that is above heaven, all that is below earth, and all that is between heaven and earth, plus what people call past, present and future, on what is all of this woven, warp and woof?"

4. Yajnavalkya answered, "All that is above heaven, all that is below earth, and all that is between heaven and earth, plus what people call past, present and future, all of this is woven warp and woof on space,[48] O Gargi."

5. "In all respects, Yajnavalkya, you have answered this question to my satisfaction. Now prepare for the next."

"Ask, O Gargi," replied Yajnavalkya.

6. Gargi continued, "Yajnavalkya, all that is above heaven, all that is below earth, and all that is between heaven and earth, plus what people call past, present and future, on what is all of this woven, warp and woof?"

7. He answered, "All that is above heaven, all that is below

[49] Verses 6 and 7 are a repetition of verses 3 and 4. This could be taken as a corruption in the text or a subtle indication of Gargi's dissatisfaction with Yajnavalkya's response the first time it was asked. It is sarcasm, and in effect she is telling Yajnavalkya to get it together and do better.
[50] Here the word *akṣara* means "non-decaying" and so the meaning is "permanent." *Kṣara,* on the other hand, means to decay, and so *akṣara* is its opposite. This physical world is sometimes called *kṣara dhama,* the realm where everything is subject to change and decay. A "spiritual" world is often called *akṣara dhama,* a place that never decays.
[51] The root word here is *aś*, to eat.
[52] This whole section is an example of describing something through negation. This is called *apoha*. For example, a cow can be described by pointing out its positive characteristics: it has a tail, it has four legs and hooves, its color is black and white, it has horns, and so on. The other way to describe a cow is through negation, by eliminating everything which is not a cow until one is left with nothing but a cow. It is not a dog, it is not blue, it does not have wings, it does not have two legs, and so on until you have removed every other possibility which is not a cow. It is common in Upanishads to use this technique of *apoha* to describe *brahma*. The famous "*neti neti neti,*" "not this, not this, not this" dictum, is also an example of *apoha*.
In addition, this section is an excellent example of alliteration. These verses were meant to be recited. And so, by combining the words with all the negative forms, a very particular sound pattern and rhythm is created.
[53] The word *praśāsana* means to rule, to have dominion and to command. This word and *vidhṛta* (see below) will be repeated many times in subsequent verses.
[54] The word is *vidhṛta,* which means to be seized, kept controlled or separated.

earth, and all that is between heaven and earth, plus what people call past, present and future, all of this, Gargi, is woven warp and woof on space."[49]

"On what, then, is space woven, warp and woof?" asked Gargi.

8. Yajnavalkya replied, "Space is woven on the Imperishable (*akṣara*).[50] The learned describe this Imperishable as not coarse or fine, not short or long, without blood or fat, and even without shadow or darkness. It is without wind, without space, without taste, and even without smell, sight or hearing. It is completely untouched by speech and mind. It is without vigor or breath or a mouth, and can never be measured inside or out. This one consumes[51] no one and no one consumes it.[52]

9. "At the command[53] of this Imperishable, Gargi, the sun and the moon are held apart.[54] At the command of this Imperishable, the heaven and earth are held apart. At the command of this Imperishable, the seconds, the hours, the days, the nights, the fortnights, the months, the seasons and the years are held apart. At the command of this Imperishable, Gargi, rivers flow from the snowcapped mountains, some going east, some going west.

10. "In this world, Gargi, if one performs sacrifice, worships, or undergoes austerities for a thousand years, it is all a waste if one does not know this Imperishable. That person is most unfortunate who leaves this world without knowing this Imperishable. On the other hand, one who knows this Imperishable upon leaving this world is a true knower of *brahma*.

11. "This Imperishable, Gargi, is the unseen seer, the unheard hearer, the unthought thinker and the unperceived perceiver. There is no other seer than this one. There is no other hearer than this one. There is no other thinker than this one. There is no other perceiver than this one. Indeed, Gargi, on this Imperishable all of space is woven, warp and woof."

12. Gargi concluded, "Learned gentlemen, consider yourself lucky if you get away from this great gentleman simply by bowing. None of you will ever defeat him in theological debate."

Thereafter Gargi became silent.

Here ends the eighth *Brāhmaṇa* of the third *Adhyāya*

Ninth *Brāhmaṇa*

The Number of Gods

1. Then Vidagdha Shakalya asked Yajnavalkya, "Pray, sir, how many gods are there?"

Yajnavalkya replied, "As many as are mentioned in the 'Eulogy

---

[55] Here the words are *vaiśva-devasya nividi*. A *nivid* is an insertion into a liturgy that contains the names of certain gods and goddesses. So this is a particular list of names found in a hymn to the Vaishva Devas.

[56] The text says 303 plus 3,003 gods, which equals 3,306.

[57] Perhaps this is nothing less than ancient humor!

[58] Again, the text reads 303 and 3,003 gods.

to the Gods,'[55] which is to say 3,306."[56]

"Indeed! But tell us, Yajnavalkya, how many gods in fact are there?"

"Thirty-three."

"Indeed! But tell us, Yajnavalkya, how many gods are there?"

"Six."

"Indeed! But tell us, Yajnavalkya, how many gods are there?"

"Three."

"Indeed! But tell us, Yajnavalkya, how many gods are there?"

"Two."

"Indeed! But really, tell us, Yajnavalkya, how many gods are there?"

"One and a half."[57]

"Indeed! But tell us, Yajnavalkya, how many gods are there?"

"One."

"Now please tell us, who are these 3,306 gods?"[58]

[59] The word is *mahiman*, which means power, greatness and majesty. Some commentators gloss this as *vibhūti*, manifestation. Compare to BG 10, Vibhuti Yoga.
[60] The word is *antarīkṣa,* which is the region of the earth's atmosphere. See BU 3.7.6 fn.
[61] There are twenty-seven *nakṣatras,* which are the daily lunar positions.
[62] The word *vasu* has multiple meanings. Not only is it the name of the gods listed here, but the word also means wealth and light. So they are the eight "wealths" of the world. In addition, the root of the word is *vas*, which means to dwell. Therefore, the Vasus are the eight dwelling places or supports of this world.
[63] Here the word is *prāṇa.* The word *prāṇa* is used in many ways throughout the Upanishads. Its primary meaning is breath, but it is also used to refer to the soul, God, the self, and the sense organs. In this case, the ten "breaths" are the five organs of cognition—the ears, eyes, nose, etc.—plus the five organs of action, the hands, the feet, etc.
[64] Here the word is *ātmā*, which could also mean the soul, the self, etc.
[65] The root of the word *rudra* is *rud*, which means to cry or lament. Therefore, a *rudra* is something that causes one to cry or lament.
[66] The sun is given a different name as it moves through each sign of the zodiac. Therefore there are twelve suns, one for each month. These are known as the Adityas. What is actually being referred to here is time, which carries away all things.
[67] The root of the word *āditya* is *ad*, which means to eat or devour. In this sense, the movement of the sun, i.e., time, eats and devours, and so in this sense carries away all things.

2. Yajnavalkya continued, "The 3,306 are the powers[59] of the gods. In fact, there are just thirty-three gods."

"And who are these thirty-three?"

2. "There are eight Vasus, eleven Rudras, and twelve Adityas, which makes thirty-one. Add to that Indra and Prajapati and you have thirty-three gods."

3. "Who are the Vasus?"

Yajnavalkya replied, "There are eight Vasus: fire, earth, wind, sky,[60] the sun, space, the moon, and the lunar mansions.[61] They are called Vasus because they are the wealth of the world.[62]

4. "Now, who are the Rudras?"

"The eleven Rudras are the ten senses[63] which reside in a person plus the mind.[64] And when these eleven Rudras leave this mortal body, they cause us to cry. Therefore they are called Rudras."[65]

5. "Who are the Adityas?"

"The Adityas are the twelve months, for they carry away the whole world.[66] That which carries away is called an Āditya."[67]

6. "Who is Indra, and who is Prajapati?"

"Indra is thunder and lightning. Prajapati is *yajña*, sacrifice."

"What is thunder and lightning?"

"The thunderbolt."

"What is sacrifice?"

"The animals that are sacrificed."

7. "Who are the six?"

Yajnavalkya replied, "Fire, earth, wind, the atmosphere region, the sun, and space are the six. They comprise this whole world."

8. "Who are the three gods?"

"The three worlds,[68] for all these gods reside in them.

"Who are the two gods?"

"Food and breath."

"Who are the one and a half gods?"

"The wind, the one who purifies."

---

[68] The three worlds are *bhūr*, *bhūva* and *suvaḥ*, which correspond respectively to the terrestrial region, the atmosphere region, and outer space.

[69] This expression, *tya*, "that yonder one," has been used previously in BU 2.3.1.

9. "Since he who purifies appears to be one, why is he called one and a half?"

"Because in him the whole world increases."

"And who is the one?"

"Breath. That yonder one,[69] *brahma*."

10. "He who truly knows that Person whose abode is the earth, whose world is fire, whose mind is light, and who is the shelter and support of all souls, that man alone, O Yajnavalkya, would be a true knower."

"Sakalya, I know that Person who is the shelter and support of all souls and of whom you speak. Yet this one who is the body, who is his god?"

"The immortal, O Yajnavalkya.

11. "He who truly knows that Person whose abode is passion, whose world is the heart, whose mind is light, and who is the shelter and support of all souls, that man alone, O Yajnavalkya, would be a true knower."

Yajnavalkya replied, "Shakalya, I know that Person who is the shelter and support of all souls of whom you speak, but this one who is immersed in passion, who is his god?"

"Women, O Yajnavalkya."

12. "He who truly knows that Person whose abode is form, whose world is the eye, whose mind is light, and who is the shelter and support of all souls, that man alone, O Yajnavalkya, would be a true knower."

Yajnavalkya replied, "Shakalya, I know that Person who is the shelter and support of all souls of whom you speak, but this person who is in the sun, who is his god?"

"Truth, O Yajnavalkya.

13. "He who truly knows that Person whose abode is space, whose world is the ear, whose mind is light, and who is the shelter and support of all souls, that man alone, Yajnavalkya, would be a true knower."

Yajnavalkya replied, "Shakalya, I know that Person who is the shelter and support of all souls of whom you speak, but the one who is in hearing and echo, and who is also a Person, who is his god?"

"The directions, O Yajnavalkya.

14. "He who truly knows that Person whose abode is darkness, whose world is the heart, whose mind is light, and who is the shelter and support of all souls, that man alone, O Yajnavalkya, would be a true knower."

Yajnavalkya replied, "Shakalya, I know that Person who is the shelter and support of all souls of whom you speak, but the one who is in darkness, and who is also a person, who is his god?"

"Death, O Yajnavalkya.

15. "He who truly knows that Person whose abode is in forms, whose world is the sight, whose mind is light, and who is the shelter and support of all souls, that man alone, O Yajnavalkya, would be a true knower."

Yajnavalkya replied, "Shakalya, I know that Person who is the shelter and support of all souls of whom you speak, but the one who is in reflection and who is also a person, who is his god?"

"Life and vitality, O Yajnavalkya.

16. "He who truly knows that Person whose abode is waters, whose world is the heart, whose mind is light, and who is the shelter and support of all souls, that man alone, O Yajnavalkya, would be a true knower."

Yajnavalkya replied, "Shakalya, I know that Person who is the shelter and support of all souls of whom you speak, but the one who is in waters and who is also a person, who is his god?"

"Varuṇa, rain, O Yajnavalkya.

17. "He who truly knows that Person whose abode is semen, whose world is the heart, whose mind is light, and who is the shelter and support of all souls, that man alone, O Yajnavalkya, would be a true knower."

Yajnavalkya replied, "Shakalya, I know that Person who is the shelter and support of all souls of whom you speak, but the one who is surrounded by sons and who is also a person, who is his god?"

"Prajapati, the progenitor, O Yajnavalkya."

18. Then Yajnavalkya asked, "Shakalya, can it be that these *brāhmanas* are simply using you to do their bidding?"[70]

Shakalya responded, "So, Yajnavalkya, what is your understanding of *brahma* that allows you to talk down these *brāhmanas* from Kuru and Pancala?"

Yajnavalkya replied, "I know the directions as well as their gods and their foundations, O Shakalya."

20. "And since you know the directions along with their gods and foundations, who is the god in the eastern direction?"

---

[70] The word is *angāravākṣayaṇa*, which is a device used to stamp out burning coals.

"The sun god, Aditya."

"On what is the sun supported?"

"On sight."

"And on what is sight supported?"

"On visible form. Sight sees visible form."

"What is the foundation of visible form?"

"The heart," replied Yajnavalkya. "For by the heart visible forms are apprehended. Therefore, form is supported in the heart."

"Indeed, you are correct, Yajnavalkya!"

21. Then Shakalya asked, "Now, according to you, who is the god in the southern direction?"

"The god of death, Yama."

"On what is Yama supported?"

"On sacrifice."

"On what is sacrifice supported?"

"On the sacrificial gift."[71]

"On what is the sacrificial gift supported, O Yajnavalkya?"

"On faith. For only when there is faith does one give the sacrificial gift. Therefore, the sacrificial gift is supported on faith."

"And on what is faith supported?"

Yajnavalkya replied, "On the heart, for one knows faith with the heart. Therefore, faith is supported in the heart."

"You are correct, Yajnavalkya!"

22. Then Shakalya asked, "Now, according to you, who is the god in the western direction?"

"The god of waters, Varuna."

"On what is Varuna supported?"

"On water."

"On what is water supported?"

---

[71] This is the gift, *dakṣinā*, given to priests at the conclusion of a sacrifice.

[72] The initiation ceremony is called *dīkṣā.*

"On semen."

"And on what is semen supported?"

"On the heart. Therefore, when a son is born who resembles the father, they say he has come from the heart. A son is created from the heart. Therefore, semen is supported from the heart."

"You are correct, Yajnavalkya!"

23. Then Shakalya asked, "Now, according to you, who is the god in the northern direction?"

"Soma, the moon god."

"On what is Soma supported?"

'On initiation."[72]

"On what is initiation supported?"

"On truth. Therefore, during initiation they say 'Speak the truth!' In this way initiation is support by truth."

"And on what is truth supported?"

"Again on the heart," replied Yajnavalkya. "For one knows truth in the heart. Therefore, truth is supported in the heart."

"You are correct, Yajnavalkya!"

24. Then Shakalya asked, "Now, according to you, who is the god at the zenith overhead?"[73]

"The fire god, Agni."

"On what is Agni supported?"

"On speech."

"On what is speech supported?"

"On the heart."

"And on what is the heart supported?"

25. At this Yajnavalkya replied, "You are such a talker, Shaka-

---

[73] Here the word is *dhruvā*, the region of the sky overhead in the vicinity of the pole star, *dhruva*.

[74] This is one of the earliest references to the five vital breaths, *prāṇas*. *Prāṇa,* for the most part, is the breath within the mouth, the main breath, but beyond that it is typically divided into five parts. While not all early sources agree on the names or number of these parts, this is one of the earliest lists and includes *prāṇa* (in-breath), *apāna* (out-breath), *vyāna* (held-breath), *udāna* (up-breath), and *samāna* (digestive energy).

[75] This again is the famous *neti neti*, "not this, not this," expression. See BU 2.3.6 for first usage and BU 4.5.15.

[76] These eight are described above in verses 10-17 of this chapter.

lya! Do you really think it is supported anywhere else than in yourself? If it were supported anywhere else than in yourself dogs would eat it and birds would tear it up!"

26. But Shakalya persisted, "On what are you and your soul supported?"

"On the incoming breath."[74]

"On what is the incoming breath supported?"

"On the outgoing breath."

"On what is the outgoing breath supported?"

"On the held-breath."

"On what is the held-breath supported?"

"On the up-breath."

"On what is the up-breath supported?"

"On the digestive breath.

"The soul is not this. The soul is not that.[75] It cannot be grasped because it does not grasp. It is indestructible because it does not destroy. It is unattached because it does not attach. It is unbound. It does not tremble. It cannot be harmed. These are the eight abodes, the eight worlds, the eight gods, and the eight persons.[76]

"I ask you about that mystical Person who brings together and then takes apart and yet who transcends these eight smaller persons. If you fail to tell me about this One, surely your head will burst!"

Shakalya did not know this One, and indeed his head did burst! Thieves even stole his bones not knowing what they were.

27. Then Yajnavalkya spoke, "Distinguished gentlemen, if you like, question me all together or alone. Or if you prefer, let me question you individually or all together." But they said nothing.

28. So finally he questioned them with these verses:

A man is like a forest tree. His hairs are the leaves and his skin is the outer bark. Pierce the skin and blood will flow, break the bark and sap will flow.

Flesh is the inner bark, fiber the muscles. The bones are the inner wood, and the pith is his marrow.

Yet a tree cut down grows again from its root. But from what root does a man, who has been cut down by death, grow?

Do not say "From his semen," because that is produced from the living. This is like saying "Having died, a tree again grows from its seed."

Only a tree that has been pulled up by the root will never grow again. So from what root does a man grow who has been cut down by death? Once born, a man is never born again. After all, who would bear him all over?

Brahma is understanding. *Brahma* is joy. *Brahma* is the ultimate goal. Brahma is the greatest gift one can give to a person determined to know.

Here ends the ninth *Brāhmaṇa* of the third *Adhyāya*

Here ends the third *Adhyāya*

Fourth *Adhyāya*

First *Brāhmaṇa*

Talks Between Janaka and Yajnavalkya

What is *Brahma*?

1. After King Janaka of Videha had been seated and the sage Yajnavalkya had arrived, Janaka addressed the sage, "Yajnavalkya, why have you come? Do you desire cows[1] or hairsplitting discussion?"

"Both, Your Majesty."

2. Yajnavalkya then continued, "So tell me, Your Majesty, what have you heard recently?"

King Janaka replied, "Jitva Shailini told me that speech itself is *brahma*."

"He told you speech itself is *brahma*? This is what anyone with a mother, a father, or a teacher might say.[2] For what else could be said by someone who has no speech? Did he tell you the source and foundation of this *brahma*?"

[1] Cows mean wealth. At these times having cows meant having wealth.

[2] This is like saying the obvious!

"He did not," replied the king.

Yajnavalkya said, "Your Majesty, this is one-footed!"[3]

"So why don't you tell us, Yajnavalkya, what you know."

"Speech is the abode of *brahma*; space[4] is its foundation. This should be respected as wisdom."

"What constitutes wisdom, Yajnavalkya?"

"Speech alone, Your Majesty. For it is through speech that relations[5] are known. It is through speech that the Rig, the Sama, the Yajur and the Atharva Vedas are known. It is through speech that the histories, the ancient lore, the sciences, the hidden teachings, the verses, the aphorisms, the explanations and the commentaries are known. It is through speech that the offerings and the oblations, the giving of food and drink, even this world and the next world, and all beings are known.[6] Speech itself is the highest *brahma*. And for one who knows and respects this, speech never leaves him. All beings surround such a person and he becomes a god. Indeed, he goes to the gods."

---

[3] Which is to say, lame.

[4] The word here is *ākāśa*, which is not outer space, but space in the sense of the distance between two objects.

[5] The word for relations is *bandhu*, which generally refers to family relations and friends.

[6] In other words, these things are the "family relations" of speech.

Being pleased, King Janaka of Videha replied, "I give you a thousand cows and a bull as powerful as an elephant."

Yajnavalkya said, "My father believed that one should not accept a gift without first teaching.

3. "So, Your Majesty, please tell us what else you have heard."

King Janaka replied, "Udanka Shaulbayana told me breath itself is *brahma*."

"He told you breath itself is *brahma*? This is what anyone with a mother, a father, or a teacher might say. For what else could be said by someone who has no breath? Did he tell you its source and foundation?"

"He did not."

Yajnavalkya replied, "Your Majesty, this is one-footed!"

"So why don't you tell us, Yajnavalkya, what you know."

"Breath is the abode of *brahma*; space is its foundation. This should be respected as the most dear."

"What constitutes the most dear, Yajnavalkya?"

"Breath alone, Your Majesty. It is for love of breath that one performs sacrifice for a person who is unworthy, and one accepts payment from such a person from whom it is forbidden to accept payment. Your Majesty, it is for the love of breath there is fear when one goes traveling.[7] Breath itself is the highest *brahma.* And for one who knows and respects this, breath never leaves him. All beings surround such a person and he becomes a god. Indeed, he goes to the gods."

Being pleased, King Janaka of Videha replied, "I give you a thousand cows and a bull as powerful as an elephant."

Yajnavalkya replied, "My father believed that one should not accept a gift without first teaching.

4. "So please tell us what else you have heard."

King Janaka replied, "Barku Varshna told me sight itself is *brahma.*"

"He told you sight itself is *brahma*? This is what anyone with a mother, a father, or a teacher might say. For what else could be said by someone who has no sight? Did he tell you its source and foundation?"

"He did not."

---

[7] In today's language we may say for the sake of a livelihood a priest performs sacrifice for an unworthy person or takes the risk of travel to perform a sacrifice.

[8] Of all the senses, eyesight is given the most importance.

Yajnavalkya replied, "Your Majesty, this is one-footed!"

"So why don't you tell us, Yajnavalkya, what you know."

"Sight is the abode of *brahma*; space is its foundation. This should be respected as truth."

"What constitutes truth, Yajnavalkya?"

"Sight alone, Your Majesty. Truly, when they say to a person who sees, 'Have you seen?' and he answers, 'I have seen,' they accept what he has seen as truth.[8] Sight itself is the highest *brahma*. And for one who knows and respects this, sight never leaves him. All beings surround such a person and he becomes a god. Indeed, he goes to the gods."

Being pleased, King Janaka of Videha replied, "I give you a thousand cows and a bull as powerful as an elephant."

Yajnavalkya replied, "My father believed that one should not accept a gift without first teaching.

5. "So please tell us what else you have heard."

King Janaka relied, "Gardabhivipita Bharadvaja told me hearing itself is *brahma*."

"He told you hearing itself is *brahma*? This is what anyone with a mother, a father, or a teacher might say. For what else could be said by someone who has no hearing? Did he tell you its source and foundation?"

"He did not."

Yajnavalkya replied, "Your majesty, this is one-footed!"

"So why don't you tell us, Yajnavalkya, what you know."

"Hearing is the abode of *brahma*; space is its foundation. This should be respected as the limitless."

"What constitutes the limitless, Yajnavalkya?"

"The directions alone, Your Majesty. Because to whatever direction a person may go, he never reaches the end. For the directions are limitless and hearing is from the directions. Hearing itself is the highest *brahma*. And for one who knows and respects this, hearing never leaves him. All beings surround such a person and he becomes a god. Indeed, he goes to the gods."

Being pleased, King Janaka of Videha replied, "I give you a thousand cows and a bull as powerful as an elephant."

Yajnavalkya replied, "My father believed that one should not accept a gift without first teaching.

6. "So please tell us what else you have heard," requested Yajnavalkya.

King Janaka replied, "Satyakama Jabala told me mind itself is *brahma*."

"He told you mind itself is *brahma*? This is what anyone with a mother, a father, or a teacher might say. For what else could be said by someone who has no mind? Did he tell you its source and foundation?"

"He did not."

Yajnavalkya replied, "Your Majesty, this is one-footed!"

"So why don't you tell us, Yajnavalkya, what you know."

"Mind is the abode of *brahma*; space is its foundation. This should be respected as joy."

"What constitutes the nature of joy, Yajnavalkya?"

"Mind alone, Your Majesty. It is through the mind that a man takes a wife and produces a son, who resembles himself. This is joy. Mind itself is the highest *brahma*. And for one who knows and respects this, mind never leaves him. All beings surround such a person and he becomes a god. Indeed, he goes to the gods."

Being pleased, King Janaka of Videha replied, "I give you a thousand cows and a bull as powerful as an elephant."

Yajnavalkya replied, "My father believed that one should not accept a gift without first teaching.

7. "So please tell us what else you have heard," inquired Yajnavalkya.

King Janaka replied, "Vidagdha Shakalya told me heart itself is *brahma*."

"He told you heart itself is *brahma*? This is what anyone with a mother, a father, or a teacher might say. For what else could be said by someone who has no heart? Did he tell you its source and foundation?"

"He did not."

Yajnavalkya replied, "Your Majesty, this is one-footed!"

"So why don't you tell us, Yajnavalkya, what you know."

"Heart is the abode of *brahma*; space is its foundation. This should be respected as stability."

"What constitutes stability, Yajnavalkya?"

"Heart alone, Your Majesty. Heart is the abode of all beings and heart is the foundation of all beings. For it is on heart that all beings are founded. Heart itself is the highest *brahma*. And for one who knows and respects this, heart never leaves him. All beings surround such a person and he becomes a god. Indeed, he goes to the gods."

Being pleased, King Janaka of Videha replied, "I give you a thousand cows and a bull as powerful as an elephant."

Yajnavalkya replied, "My father believed that one should not accept a gift without first teaching."

Here ends the first *Brāhmaṇa* of the fourth *Adhyāya*

Second *Brāhmaṇa*

Talks between Janaka and Yajnavalkya Continued
The Destination of the Soul

1. King Janaka of Videha then got down from his royal seat and approached Yajnavalkya, the learned sage, and said, "All respects to you, Yajnavalkya! Please instruct me."

Yajnavalkya replied, "As a great king who is about to undertake a journey will take a chariot or ship, you have equipped yourself with these mystic teachings. So you are famous, wealthy, and learned in the Vedas, and you have heard these mystic teachings. Now tell me, where will you go when you leave this world?"

"That, good sir, I do not know," replied the king.

"Then let me tell you," said Yajnavalkya.

"Yes, please tell me, good sir," replied the king.

2. "The name of the person in the right eye is Indha.[9] Yet even though his true name is Indha, people indirectly call him Indra, for the gods love the indirect and dislike the direct.[10]

3. "His wife, Virat, is the person in the left eye. Their meeting place is the area around the heart. Their food is the red ball of the heart. Their clothes are the weblike substance around the heart. Their pathway is the main vein that goes up from the heart. Like hair that has been split a thousandfold, there are *hitās,* fine veins and nerves, which are found around the heart. Through these nourishment flows and, because of that, they receive better food than the body itself.[11]

4. "The forward-facing vital functions[12] constitute the eastern

---

[9] The person in the eye is the pupil of the eye. Also see fn to BU 2.3.4.

[10] We see this even today, where a king or judge is addressed indirectly, as Your Majesty or Your Honor.

[11] The meaning of this section is obscure. Perhaps it is a reference to the relationship between the subtle (astral) body and the physical body.

[12] Here the word is *prāṇa,* and it can be understood as the vital functions of the body.

[13] This is the famous *neti, neti, neti* expression used throughout the Upanishads. For the first usage see BU 2.3.6 fn.

[14] Literally, "Here are the people of Videha, here am I."

[15] The religious gathering was an *agni-hotra*. There is reference to this gathering in the SB 11.6.2.10. At that time the sage had given the king the favor that he could ask any question he wished. Now the king decided to exercise that favor.

direction. The right-side vital functions constitute the southern direction. The back-facing vital functions constitute the western direction. The left-side vital functions constitute the northern direction. The upper-facing vital functions constitute the zenith, and the lower-side vital functions constitute the nadir. In this way, the vital functions are related to all the directions.

"The *ātmā* is not this, the *ātmā* is not that.[13] It cannot be grasped because it is ungraspable. It cannot be destroyed because it is indestructible. It is unattached because it does not attach. It is unbound. It is never afflicted, and neither can it be harmed. Janaka, indeed you have attained fearlessness," said Yajnavalkya.

Janaka of Videha replied, "Respected Yajnavalkya, you have made us know fearlessness! May fearlessness know you. All respects to you! These people of Videha and myself are at your service."[14]

Here ends the second *Brāhmaṇa* of the fourth *Adhyāya*

Third *Brāhmaṇa*

Talks Between Janaka and Yajnavalkya Continued
The Light of Man

1. Yajnavalkya went to King Janaka of Videha intending to be silent. However, the sage had given the king a favor when they had once been together at a religious gathering.[15] At that time King Janaka chose to ask anything he wished. Yajnavalkya had agreed, so now the king asked:

2. "Yajnavalkya, what is the light of man?"

"The sun, Your Majesty. For it is by the light of the sun that a man sits, goes about, works, and returns," the sage replied.

"Indeed, this is true," said the king.

3. "But after the sun has set, what is the light of man?"

"The moon is his light. For it is by the light of the moon that a man sits, goes about, works, and returns."

"Indeed, this is true," said the king.

4. "But after both the sun and the moon have set, what is the light of man?"

"Fire is his light. For it is by the light of fire that a man sits, goes about, works, and returns."

"Indeed, this is true," said the king.

5. "But after both the sun and the moon have set, and fire has been extinguished, what is the light of man?"

---

[16] This sentence can also be read "What is the *ātmā*?"

[17] The word is *vijñāna*, which is also understanding, discrimination, intelligence and even knowledge.

[18] This world and the world beyond. See vs 9.

"Speech is his light. For it is by the light of speech that he sits, goes about, works, and returns. Therefore, Your Majesty, when a man cannot see even his hand because of darkness he goes to where sound is heard."

"Indeed, this is true," said the king.

6. "But after both the sun and the moon have set, fire has been extinguished, and speech has been silenced, what is the light of man?"

"The *ātmā* is his light. For it is by the light of the *ātmā* that he sits, goes about, works, and returns," replied Yajnavalkya.

7. "Who is this *ātmā*?" asked the king.[16]

"Amongst all the *prāṇas,* the *ātmā* is the one that consists of intellect.[17] It is the spirit, who is the light within the heart. It is the one who travels equally between these two worlds.[18] It is the one who thinks and moves about, and upon falling asleep it is the one who transcends this world and all of its forms of death.

8. "When a person is born, he assumes a body and thereby comes into contact with evil; and then, at death, as he departs this world, he gives up this evil.

9. "This person exists in two worlds: the world here and the world beyond. Yet there is a third world, which is in-between:

the world of dreams.[19] While in this in-between world, one can see both the world here and the world beyond. This dream world is a doorway into that world beyond. As one approaches that world beyond, one can see both the evils of the world here and the joys of that world beyond.

"As a man dreams, he takes all the things of the waking world, disassembles them, and then reassembles them in his own way to create a new world, and so in his dream world he shines by his own light.

10. "In his dream world there are no chariots, no teams of horses, and no roads. Yet he creates chariots, teams of horses and roads. In his dream world there are no joys, no pleasures and no delights. Yet he creates joys and pleasures and delights. In his dream world there are no ponds, no lakes and no rivers. Yet he creates ponds, lakes and rivers. This is because the dreaming person is the creator of his own world."

---

[19] The expression is *svapna-sthāna*, which is the place of *svapna*. *Svapna* can be either sleep or dream.

[20] The Sanskrit is *eka-hamsa*, lone swan. Here the reference is to the astral body.

[21] These verses appear to describe how the subtle astral body leaves the gross physical body during sleep and travels at will.

[22] What is implied here is that the things of the dream world are not actually there, so it is only by the dreamer's own light that the things of the dream world exist.

11. In this regard there are the following verses:

Overpowering all parts of the body by sleep,
The unsleeping one looks down upon the sleeping one.
Full of light, the golden one, this lone swan,[20]
Returns again to his place.

12. Protecting his lower resting place by breath,
This immortal one rises up from its resting place.
This golden one, the lone swan, then
Roams at will according to his desires.

13. In his dreaming state, going high and low,
This god creates unlimited forms—
Enjoying women,
Laughing,
Even seeing fearful things.

14. While they see this—his garden of pleasures—
Who truly sees him?[21]

"They say one should never awaken a sleeping person, for it is difficult to cure one who has not returned. They also say his dream world is his waking world because, in his dream world, he sees the same things as in his waking world. Yet in this dream world, a person shines by his own light."[22]

King Janaka said, "Good sir! For this I will give you a thousand cows![23] But you'll have to tell me something higher for my release."[24]

15. "In reposed dream sleep[25] this person moves about, enjoys, sees good and evil, and then returns to his dream state. Whatever he saw or whatever he did in this reposed dream sleep does not stay with him because nothing attaches to this person."

The king said, "This is true, Yajnavalkya! For this I give you a thousand cows! But you'll have to tell me something even higher for my release."

16. Yajnavalkya continued, "Then, in dream sleep this person

---

[23] The text literally says a thousand. There is no mention of cows. The context suggests cows.

[24] Janaka had a favor from Yajnavalkya that he could ask any question, so here the king is reminding the sage that he still must speak more before the king would consider him released from his favor. Others take this to mean "release from rebirth."

[25] Four levels of consciousness are mentioned in this section: a form of deep dream sleep that is here called reposed dream sleep (*samprasāda*), dream sleep (*svapna*), wakefulness (*buddhānta*), and then a state of deep sleep wherein everything is forgotten (*supta*). Here the person is shown to move regularly through these four levels of consciousness.

[26] Previous references in this Upanishad to these *hitās* are BU 2.1.19, 4.2.3. Other references can be found in CU 8.6.1 and MU 1.2.11. These *hitās* are also called *nādis,* and they are pathways through which the subtle astral body travels. See also BU 4.4.9 for reference to these colors.

moves about, enjoys, sees good and evil, and then returns to his awakened state. Whatever he saw or whatever he did in this dream sleep does not stay with him because nothing attaches to this person."

The king said, "This is true, Yajnavalkya! For this I give you a thousand cows! But you'll have to tell me something even higher for my release."

17. Again Yajnavalkya continued, "Then, in his awakened state this person moves about, enjoys, sees good and evil, and then returns to his dream sleep.

18. "Consider this: As a great fish moves back and forth between two shores—the far shore and the near shore—so a person moves back and forth between these two states, dream sleep and wakefulness.

19. "Consider this: As a great falcon flying in the sky becomes tired and so folds its wings and lands in its nest, so a person moves to that state of deep sleep wherein he desires nothing and sees no dream.

20. "This person has subtle pathways called *hitās,* which are like hairs split a thousandfold and which are colored white, blue, orange, green and red.[26] Sometimes, in his dreams, out of ignorance, he imagines he has been killed or vanquished or is being chased by an elephant or has fallen into a pit; but these are only fears he has seen in his awakened state. Then there are other

times when he imagines he has become a god or a king, and so thinks, 'All this I am!' At this time he is on the top of his world.

21. "Then there is his state beyond all worldly desires, free of evil and without fear.

"Consider this: As a man who is locked in a deep embrace with his lover is oblivious to everything, so one who is locked in deep meditation with the all-conscious *ātmā* is oblivious to everything both inside and out. Indeed, this is the state wherein all desires have been fulfilled, where the *ātmā* is the only focus and where one is free of worldly desire or sorrow.

22. "In this state a father is not a father, a mother is not a mother, the worlds are not worlds, gods are not gods, and the Vedas are not Vedas. In this state a thief is not a thief, a murderer is not murderer,[27] an outcast is not an outcast,[28] a mixed breed is not a mixed breed,[29] a mendicant is not a mendicant, and an ascetic is not an ascetic. In this state one is not affected by good or evil for this person has surpassed all sorrows of the heart.

---

[27] Here the word is *bhrūṇa-hā,* which is literally a killer of *bhrūṇa.* A *bhrūṇa* is either a fetus or a *brāhmaṇa.*

[28] Here the word is *cāṇḍāla*, which is technically a child born of a *śudra* father and a *brāhmaṇa* mother.

[29] Here the word is *paulkaśa*, which is technically a child born of a *śudra* father and a *kṣatriya* mother.

[30] The Sanskrit literally says "There is no second."

23. "In this state he does not see, yet still he sees, though he does not see what is usually seen. For the seer never ceases to see. This is because the *ātmā* is imperishable and there is nothing separate[30] from the *ātmā* that could be seen.

24. "In this state he does not smell, yet still he smells, though he does not smell what is usually smelled. For the seer never ceases to smell. This is because the *ātmā* is imperishable and there is nothing separate from the *ātmā* that could be smelled.

25. "In this state he does not taste, yet still he tastes, though he does not taste what is usually tasted. For the taster never ceases to taste. This is because the *ātmā* is imperishable and there is nothing separate from the *ātmā* that could be tasted.

26. "In this state he does not speak, yet still he speaks, though he does not speak what is usually spoken. For the speaker never ceases to speak. This is because the *ātmā* is imperishable and there is nothing separate from the *ātmā* that could be spoken.

27. "In this state he does not hear, yet still he hears, though he does not hear what is usually heard. For the hearer never ceases to hear. This is because the *ātmā* is imperishable and there is nothing separate from the *ātmā* that could be heard.

28. "In this state he does not think, yet still he thinks, though he does not think what is usually thought. For the thinker never ceases to think. This is because the *ātmā* is imperishable and there is nothing separate from the *ātmā* that could be thought.

29. "In this state he does not touch, yet still he touches, though he does not touch what is usually touched. For the seer never ceases to touch. This is because the *ātmā* is imperishable and there is nothing separate from the *ātmā* that could be touched.

30. "In this state he does not know, yet still he knows, though he does not know what is usually known. For the knower never ceases to know. This is because the *ātmā* is imperishable and there is nothing separate from the *ātmā* that could be known.

31. "Only when there is an 'other' can something be seen.[31] Only when there is an 'other' can something be smelled. Only when there is an 'other' can something be tasted. Only when there is an 'other' can something be spoken. Only when there is an 'other' can something be heard. Only when there is an 'other' can something be thought. Only when there is an 'other' can something be touched. Only when there is an 'other' can something be known.

---

[31] For example, high only has meaning if there is low. This idea is developed in the next chapter. (BU 4.4.2)

[32] The word used here is *dvaita*, duality.

[33] In later Hinduism the Gandharvas are a class of celestial beings regarded as singers and musicians. They dwell in the sky. In the RV there is one Gandharva who is associated with the moon and who is the protector of the *soma* elixir. Here the reference seems to suggest the later perspective.

32. "As a vast body of water is one, a seer who enters this state ceases to see the 'other.'[32] Your Majesty, this is the world of *brahma*."

Thus Yajnavalkya instructed the king. This teaching is the highest goal, the highest wealth, the highest world, and the highest joy. All beings exist on just a tiny measure of this joy!

33. "That person amongst all men who is accomplished and wealthy, who rules over all, and who enjoys all pleasures humanly possible, experiences the highest joys of human life. A hundred measures of such human enjoyment compare to just one measure of enjoyment experienced by one who has attained the world of the forefathers. A hundred measures of such joys experienced by those in the world of the forefathers compare to just one measure of joy for one who dwells in the world of the Gandharvas.[33] A hundred measures of such joy experienced by those in the world of the Gandharvas compare to just one measure of joy for one who has attained the world of the gods through good deeds. A hundred measures of such joy experienced by those who have attained the world of the gods through good deeds compare to just one measure of joy for one who has attained the world of the gods through birth, including those who are learned, straightforward, or unaffected by desire. A hundred measures of such joy experienced by those who have attained the world of the gods through birth compare to just one measure of joy for one who has attained the world of the Prajapatis, including those who are learned, straightforward, or unaffected by desire. A hundred measures of such joy experienced

by those have attained the world of the Prajapatis compare to just one measure of joy for one who has attained the world of *brahma,*[34] including those who are learned, straightforward, or unaffected by desire. The joy of the world of *brahma*, Your Majesty, is indeed the highest pleasure of all."

Thus spoke Yajnavalkya.

"For this, good sir, I give you a thousand cows! But still you'll have to tell me something even higher for my release," said the king.

---

[34] Here the expression is *brahma-lokah*, and the *brahma* that is meant here could either be the god Brahmā or *brahma* that has been mentioned throughout this Upanishad. There are two words, *Brahmā* and *brahma,* and they both look the same in their stem form (*brahman*), yet one is masculine and the other is neuter. The masculine form declines as *brahmā* and it means the creator god, Brahmā. The neuter form declines as *brahma* and means God as the impersonal "force" that has been used throughout this Upanishad. It is always a debate whether the god Brahmā is meant or *brahma,* God as force, is meant.

[35] There are two *ātmās* mentioned here, one the physical body and the other the subtle astral body. In essence, what is being described is how the physical body is like a cart loaded with a subtle body that, over a lifetime, gets loaded up with all the experiences, both good and bad, of life.

[36] The word is *aṇimāna*, which literally means fineness or lightness.

[37] Specifically, the fruit of the mango, fig and berry trees are mentioned.

[38] The word is *prāṇa*, breath or life. This should not necessarily be understood as a reference to reincarnation. This could just as likely be a reference to *pitṛ loka*, being born as a forefather.

At this Yajnavalkya became fearful and thought, "This king is sharp. He has flushed me out of every place."

34. So Yajnavalkya continued, "After that person has enjoyed and traveled about, and seen good and evil in his dream world, he finally rushes back to his source in the same way he came and enters once again into his waking state.

35. "As a loaded cart creaks along, so this physical body loaded with the experienced subtle body[35] creaks along until it breathes its last.

36. "As he becomes feeble,[36] whether from old age or disease, this person becomes freed from the body just as the fruit of a tree[37] falls to the ground, enters its source, and returns to new vitality.[38]

37. "Just as village leaders, magistrates, police officers and charioteers wait with food, drink and lodging for an approaching king, and call out 'He is coming, he is coming!' so all beings wait for this learned one and call out '*Brahma* is coming, *brahma* is coming.'

38. "Just as village leaders, magistrates, police officers and charioteers gather around a king at the time of his death, so all the vital elements gather around this departing soul as he breathes his last."

Thus ends the third *Brāhmaṇa* of the fourth *Adhyāya*

Fourth *Brāhmaṇa*

Talks Between Janaka and Yajnavalkya Continued

The Process of Dying

1. Yajnavalkya continued, "As a dying man weakens, he loses consciousness and his vital functions (*prāṇas*) gather around him. A measure of his energy descends to his heart, and as the person in the eye turns away, he is no longer able to see form.

---

[39] In the previous chapter (BU 4.3.31) the idea was presented that in order to see, hear, smell, etc., there had to be an "other." In other words, duality is necessary for cognition. One cannot perceive high unless there is a low. So as the dying person enters *brahma,* duality slips away and he loses the "other," and so he ceases to perceive.

[40] Sometimes it is said at the moment of death one's whole life flashes before the person. This reference suggests the same.

[41] The Sanskrit is *avidyāṃ gamayitvā,* which is literally "causing ignorance to go." Some render this as "going to unconsciousness," that the soul strikes down the body and renders it unconscious.

[42] Some translators take this as "As a weaver takes a measure of cloth…" It is common that gold threads are woven into cloth, so this is likely the connection with gold and cloth.

[43] The word is *prājāpatya.* The *prajāpatis* are a class of semi divine beings charged with populating the universe.

[44] Two pronouns are used here, *idam* and *adah,* meaning the "this here" and the "this over there." The "this here" can be taken as the *ātmā,* or even this world. The "this over there" can be taken as *brahma.* There is a similar usage of *idam* and *adaḥ* in the famous *Oṃ pūrṇam adaḥ pūrṇam idam* verse in the Isha Upanishad (Invocation). Also see BU 2.3.1 fn.

2. "So people say, 'He is becoming one, he cannot see! He is becoming one, he cannot smell! He is becoming one, he cannot taste! He is becoming one, he cannot speak! He is becoming one, he cannot hear! He is becoming one, he cannot think! He is becoming one, he cannot touch! He is becoming one, he cannot understand!'[39] At that point the core of his heart lights up and the *ātmā* leaves through the eye, the head, or some other part of the body. And as that happens the vital breaths depart, after which the other vital functions depart and he becomes mere awareness. And as awareness departs he becomes seized by the memories of his past actions.[40]

3. "Consider this: As a caterpillar reaches the tip of a blade of grass and contracts itself to cross over to another blade, so the soul relinquishes this body, dispels its ignorance,[41] contracts itself and reaches out for a new life.

4. "Consider this: As a goldsmith takes a measure of gold[42] and uses it to make something new and more beautiful, so the soul relinquishes this body, dispels its ignorance, and creates a new and more beautiful form, such as a *pitri*, a *gandharva*, a god or goddess, a progenitor,[43] or some other divine being.

5. "Indeed, this *ātmā* is *brahma,* which comprises all things: consciousness, mind, breath, sight, hearing, earth, water, wind, space, heat, cold, desire, non-desire, anger, non-anger, justice and injustice. Therefore, there is the saying 'It is made of this; It is made of that.'[44]

"A person becomes who he is by how he acts and conducts oneself. If one does good, one becomes good. If one does evil, one becomes evil. Good comes from good actions, evil comes from evil actions. Indeed, they say a person is solely made of desire. So how a person desires creates one's resolve, and how a person resolves creates one's plan of actions, and how one acts creates what a person becomes.

6. "In this regard there is the following verse:

'To where the mind and the subtle body cling,
The attached soul goes along with its deeds.

'Exhausting the fruits of his action for whatever he has done,
This soul once again returns to this world of action from that world.'[45]

"This is the situation for the soul who desires.

"Now, for the soul who does not desire—who is without desire, whose desires are fulfilled and who desires the *ātmā* alone—his

---

[45] This appears to be a reference to reincarnation.
[46] Literally, his vital breaths never depart.
[47] Here the Sanskrit is *svagaṃ lokam*, "heavenly realm." This could be interpreted as the highest level of heaven or as "beyond heaven," namely liberation.
[48] Under BU 4.3.20 a similar color pattern is mentioned relating to the *hitās*.

life is never wasted.[46] Such a one is *brahma* and so goes to *brahma.*

7. "In this regard there is the following verse:

'When all the desire contained within the heart has been given up, at that time this mortal one becomes immortal and reaches *brahma.*'

"As a snake skin is thrown off and lays discarded on an anthill, so lays this discarded body. Yet the vital life force is bodiless and immortal. It verily is *brahma*, it is light."

King Janaka of Videha said, "Good sir! For this I will give you a thousand cows!"

Yajnavalkya continued: In this regard there are the following verses:

8. There is an ancient and subtle path which extends beyond this world. I have discovered and touched this path. Those wise ones, the *brahma*-knowers, who are released from this world travel this path to the heavenly realms.[47]

9. They say the colors on this path are white, blue, orange, green, and red.[48] This path was first discovered by a *brahma*-knower, and the shinning ones, the doers of good, follow this path.

[49] This verse is identical with IU 9. Literally, *vidyā* is knowledge and *avidyā* is the opposite, non-knowledge or ignorance. So in this verse, if we translate *avidyā* as ignorance, then it makes reasonable sense to translate the first part as "Those who are intent upon **ignorance** enter blinding darkness." But to translate the second half as "but those who delight in **knowledge** enter an even greater darkness" makes no sense. How can knowledge lead to an even worst situation than ignorance? This problem forces the commentator to come up with an explanation. One explanation is to say that the text is corrupt, another is to change the meaning of *avidyā* and *vidyā*. Instead of ignorance and knowledge, I prefer "material knowledge" and "spiritual knowledge." That is to say, knowledge of practical things like architecture, medicine, plumbing, etc., and knowledge of metaphysical things like the soul and God.

Regardless of how we translate *vidyā* and *avidyā,* we must understand that they are opposites and so, according to this Upanishad, both sides of life, the spiritual and the material, need to be utilized to achieve the successful life. What comprises complete knowledge, therefore, is the combination of both *vidyā* and *avidyā*. To regard practical knowledge as a form of ignorance or somehow inferior is wrong, and to think that one can survive on spiritual knowledge alone is also wrong. Spiritual knowledge understood as knowledge of the soul and God is incomplete; practical knowledge understood as knowledge of hygiene, architecture, medicine, etc. is also incomplete. Even a *yogī,* a monk, needs a place to live, food, protection and hygiene, etc., all things derived from *avidyā*, practical knowledge. So the combination of both *avidyā* and *vidyā* creates complete knowledge and, dare I say it, civilization.

[50] This verse is identical with IU 3.

10. Those who are intent upon *avidyā* enter dense darkness, but those who delight in *vidyā* enter an even greater darkness.[49]

11. Joyless are those worlds of dense darkness. Persons who live in ignorance and who are unconscious enter these worlds after death.[50]

12. Yet if a person should come to know the *ātmā* so he can truly say "I am this one," what could he desire, or who could he love, that could cause him to want to remain suffering in this body?

13. Indeed, one who has discovered and realized this *ātmā,* even though he has entered into this dense bodily realm, becomes the author of his destiny. The world belongs to him. Truly, he is the world!

14. Even while living in this body, it is possible to know the *ātmā.* But if one fails to gain this knowledge, his destruction will be great. Those who come to know this One become immortal, but those who fail are overtaken by the sorrows of this world.

15. The person who clearly sees this shining *ātmā*, the Lord of what has been and what will be, no longer hides himself from this One.

16. The gods revere this Lord as the Immortal, the Light of lights and the One before whom the years with their days revolve.

17. That One in which the five,[51] along with space, are established I take to be the *ātmā*. I have attained this knowledge. I have attained immortality, and I believe this One to be the *ātmā*, the immortal *brahma*.

18. One who knows the Breather behind breath, the Seer behind sight, the Hearer behind hearing, the Thinker behind thought, has realized this immortal and primal *brahma*.

19. Here is something that must be considered: There is no diversity[52] in this world, yet one who thinks he sees such diversity simply travels from one death to another.

20. This *ātmā* must be seen as a oneness, imperishable, fixed, pure, beyond space, unborn, immense and immovable.

21. Through study and introspection let the determined *brahma*-knower gradually gain insight. Let him not reflect with too many words for this only becomes a waste of speech.

---

[51] Commentators offer various possibilities as to what the group of five may be. One suggestion is Gandharvas, ancestors, gods, *asuras* and *rakṣasas*. Another is the five senses. Yet another is the four *varṇas* plus outcastes.

[52] Here the word for diversity is *nānā*, which means differences, variegation, and plurality. So it means that a person who only sees the variegation of this world and so fails to see the underlying substratum, *brahma,* is condemned to repeated death.

[53] Here the Sanskrit is the famous "*neti neti*" expression.
See 2.3.6 fn.

22. Of all the vital functions, this immense and unborn *ātmā* is the one full of consciousness. He is the Lord and Controller who resides within the heart. He is not increased by good actions, nor is He diminished by evil actions. He is the Master, the Governor and the King of all beings. He is the embankment keeping these worlds from touching. He is the One *brahma*-knowers desire to know through repetition of mantras, sacrifice, charity, austerity, and even through great and terrible fasting. Upon knowing Him one becomes a sage. Ascetics travel this world desiring to know Him.

In the past the wise understood this and so they gave up the desire for offspring. Instead they thought, "What is the use of worldly things? We have the *ātmā,* so this is our world." Consequently, they rose above the desire for sons, wealth and land, and so adopted the life of the mendicant. Again they thought, "This desire for sons is simply the desire for wealth. The desire for wealth is simply the desire for lands. Both are but desires."

Concerning this *ātmā,* all that can truly be said is "It is not this, it is not that."[53] This *ātmā* cannot be grasped; therefore, it is ungraspable. It cannot be destroyed; therefore, it is indestructible. Nothing attaches to it; therefore, it can never be adhered to. It is unfettered, without fear, and can never be harmed. The thoughts "I have done evil; I have done good" never arise. This *ātmā* is beyond these thoughts and is never touched by what has been done or what has been left undone.

23. Consider the following verse:

This *ātmā* is the eternal greatness of a *brahma*-knower.
It is never increased or diminished by action. Learn to see its signs. Know it and you will never be tainted by evil.

Understanding this, the *brahma*-knower becomes calm, restrained, detached, patient and composed. He sees the *ātmā* in himself and in others. The *brahma*-knower is untouched by evil and so he overcomes all evil. It never scorches him; in fact, he burns evil. The *brahma*-knower is sinless and without stain and

---

[54] A similar discussion has been seen previously in BU 2.4.

[55] Here Maitreyi is described as a *brahma-vādinī*, literally a "discourser on the subject of *brahma*," whereas Katyayani is described as *strī-prajñā eva,* "only having the realization of a woman." That Yajnavalkya had two wives with opposite interests is significant. Maitreyi was keenly interested in *vidyā,* spiritual knowledge, while Katyayani was solely taken by *avidyā*, worldly knowledge. That both were the wives of the sage suggests that both *vidyā* and *avidyā* are required for success. One needs both spiritual knowledge as well as practical, material knowledge in order to live a happy life. The Isha Upanishad also makes this point. (See IU 11: "One who possesses both matter and spirit with matter transcends death and with spirit attains immortality.") Earlier in this Upanishad we saw Yajnavalkya contesting for the wealth of cows and gold, his Katyayani side, so to speak. Yet now that Yajnavalkya had reached the end of his householder life, he was preparing to move on to a new stage, as described in the next verse. This is his Maitreyi side.

[56] Yajnavalkya had completed his householder life and was preparing to adopt his final stage as a *sannyasī* or mendicant. Before he left the world, he wanted to divide his wealth between his two wives.

[57] These verses show how women had equal rights to education and inheritance.

so becomes free of doubt. Your Majesty, I have thus brought you to the *brahma*-knower's world. Thus spoke Yajnavalkya.

The King replied, "Honorable sir! I present myself and all the citizens of Videha as your servants."

24. Yajnavalkya concluded, "This *ātmā* is immense and unborn. It is the eater of food and the giver of wealth. One who understands this gains wealth."

25. Indeed, this immense, unborn, ageless, undying, immortal and fearless *ātmā* is *brahma*. And because *brahma* is without fear, the one who truly understands this also become fearless.

Thus ends the fourth *Brāhmaṇa* of the fourth *Adhyāya*

Fifth *Brāhmaṇa*

Talks between Yajnavalkya and Maitreyi

1. Yajnavalkya had two wives, Maitreyi and Katyayani.[54] Maitreyi was a seeker of sacred knowledge, whereas Katyayani simply had the usual interests in life.[55] So as Yajnavalkya was preparing to undertake a new status in life,[56] he spoke.

2. "My dear Maitreyi I am going to renounce the world, so I'd like to make a settlement between you and Katyayani."[57]

3. Maitreyi asked, "If I possessed all the wealth and pleasures of the world, would I have immortality?"

"Certainly not," replied Yajnavalkya. "You would simply have a life of all things. There is no hope of immortality through wealth."

4. Maitreyi replied, "Then what is the use of things that do not lead to immortality? Instead, good sir, please share your knowledge with me."

5. Yajnavalkya said, "O noble lady, you have always been most dear to me, but now you have become even more dear. Indeed, I will explain it all to you! So as I speak, please consider what I say with concentration."

6. Yajnavalkya began, "A husband is dear not for love of husband, but for the love of *ātmā*. A wife is dear not for love of wife, but for the love of *ātmā*. Sons are dear not for love of sons, but for the love of *ātmā*. Wealth is dear not for love of wealth, but for the love of *ātmā*. Livestock is dear not for love of livestock, but for the love of *ātmā*. The *brāhmana* is dear not for love of *brāhmana*, but for the love of *ātmā*. The *kṣatriya* is dear not for love of *kṣatriya*, but for the love of *ātmā*. These worlds are dear not for love of worlds, but for the love of *ātmā*. The

---

[58] In later Hinduism a similar succession has been repeated except *ātmā* has been replaced by *hari-kathā*, hearing the stories of Krishna. It is *hari-kathā* that should be heard, discerned, meditated upon, etc. See Bhag 1/19/38.

[59] The idea is that the *ātmā* cannot be understood directly. Yet by understanding the nature of the physical world, one can achieve an understanding of the *ātmā*. There is a relationship between the two.

gods are dear not for love of gods, but for the love of *ātmā*. The Vedas are dear not for love of Vedas, but for the love of *ātmā*. Beings are dear not for love of beings, but for the love of *ātmā*. All things are dear not for love of all things, but for the love of *ātmā*. My dear Maitreyi, it is *ātmā* that should be seen, it is *ātmā* that should be heard, it is *ātmā* that should be considered, and it is *ātmā* that should be discerned. For by seeing, hearing, considering, and discerning *ātmā,* all this world can be known.[58]

7. "True priestly power evades one who thinks priestly power is anything other than *ātmā*. True royal power evades one who thinks royal power is anything other than *ātmā*. The worlds evade one who thinks the worlds are anything other than *ātmā*. The gods evade one who thinks the gods are anything other than *ātmā.* The Vedas evade one who thinks the Vedas are anything other than *ātmā.* Beings evade one who thinks beings are anything other than *ātmā.* All things evade one who thinks all things are anything other than *ātmā*. For priestly power, royal power, these worlds, the gods, the Vedas, all beings, and indeed, all things are nothing but *ātmā*.

8. "Consider this: The external sound of a drum can never be seized. Yet by seizing the drum or the drummer, that same sound can be seized.[59]

9. "The external sound of a conch can never be seized. Yet by seizing the shell or the blower, that same sound can be seized.

10. "The sound of a vina can never be seized. Yet by seizing the

vina or the player, that same sound can be seized.

11. "As different kinds of smoke billow up from green wood placed on a fire, so from the breathing of this Great Being the Rig, Yajur, Sama and Atharva Vedas, the histories, the Puranas, the sciences, the Upanishads, verses, aphorisms, explanations, commentaries, sacrifices, oblations, offerings of food and drink, and even this world, the next world, and all beings issue forth from the breathing of this Great Being.

12. "As the ocean is the meeting place[60] of all waters, so the skin is the meeting place of all sensations, the nose is the meeting place of all scents, the tongue is the meeting place of all flavors, the eye is the meeting place of all form, the ear is the meeting place of all sounds, the mind is the meeting place of all conceptions, the heart is the meeting place of all knowledge, the hands are the meeting place of all actions, the genitals are the meeting place of pleasure, the anus is the meeting place of all evacuations, the feet are the meeting place of journeys, and

---

[60] The word here is *ekāyana*, comprised of *eka+ ayana*, literally meaning "going to one." "Convergence"could be a possible rendering.

[61] The Sanskrit is *prajñāna-ghana*, literally a "mass of cognition." This is the source of the later tradition that uses the expression *sat cit ānanda* to define the qualities of God and the soul. There *cit* describes the "all-knowing" characteristics. So as salt is nothing but saltiness through and through, so the *ātmā* is nothing but cognition through and through.

[62] The word is *saṃjñā*, consciousness or cognition.

[63] See BU 2.3.6 fn and BU 3.9.26.

speech is the meeting place of all the Vedas.

13. "As sea salt is just salt, both inside and outside, so this *ātmā* is simply cognition[61] inside and out. Arising from the assembly of these elements, this *ātmā* similarly vanishes with the dissolution of these elements. My dear, I say there is no consciousness[62] after death." Thus spoke Yajnavalkya.

14. Maitreyi then asked, "Most honorable sir, I am confused. I simply do not understand."

Yajnavalkya replied, "I have said nothing confusing, my dear. This *ātmā* is indestructible. In fact, its very nature is indestructibility.

15. "But when one sees duality, one sees 'the other,' one smells 'the other,' one tastes 'the other,' one speaks of 'the other,' one hears 'the other,' one thinks of 'the other,' one touches 'the other,' and one understands 'the other.' But when only the *ātmā* is perceived—when there is no duality—by who or what can one see, smell, taste, hear, think, touch, or understand? Indeed, who can know anything of this world? About the *ātmā* all we can say is 'It is not this, it is not that.'[63] And because it is ungraspable, it cannot be grasped. Because it is non-decaying, it never decays. Because it cannot be adhered to, it does not adhere to anything. It is unbounded. It does not fear. It can never be injured. When there is no 'other,' how can a perceiver ever be known? My dear Maitreyi, you have been instructed! There is nothing more to say about immortality."

Thus speaking, Yajnavalkya departed.

Thus ends the fifth *Brāhmaṇa* of the fourth *Adhyāya*

Sixth *Brāhmaṇa*

The Lineage of Teachers and Students[64]

1. Now the lineage of teachers:
Pautimāṣya received this teaching from Gaupavana,
Gaupavana from Pautimāṣya,
Pautimāṣya from Gaupavana,
Gaupavana from Kauśika,
Kauśika from Kauṇḍinya,
Kauṇḍinya from Śāṇḍilya,
Śāṇḍilya from Kauśika and Gautama,
Gautama (2) from Āgniveśya,
Āgniveśya from Gārgya,
Gārgya from Gārgya,
Gārgya from Gautama,
Gautama from Saitava,
Saitava from Pārāśaryāyaṇa,
Pārāśaryāyaṇa from Gārgyāyaṇa,
Gārgyāyaṇa from Uddālakāyana,
Uddālakāyana from Jābālāyana,
Jābālāyana from Mādhyaṃdināyana,
Mādhyaṃdināyana from Saukarāyaṇa,

---

[64] There are two other such lists in this Upanishad. See BU 2.6 and BU 6.5.

Saukarāyaṇa from Kāśāyaṇa,
Kāśāyaṇa from Sāyakāyana,
Sāyakāyana from Kauśikāyani,
Kauśikāyani (3) from Ghṛtakauśika,
Ghṛtakauśika from Pārāśaryāyaṇa,
Pārāśaryāyaṇa from Pārāśarya,
Pārāśarya from Jātūkarṇya,
Jātūkarṇya from Āsurāyana and Yāska,
Āsurāyana from Traivaṇi,
Traivaṇi from Aupajandhani,
Aupajandhani from Āsuri,
Āsuri from Bhāradvāja,
Bhāradvāja from Ātreya,
Ātreya from Māṇṭi,
Māṇṭi from Gautama,
Gautama from Gautama,
Gautama from Vātsya,
Vātsya from Śāṇḍilya,
Śāṇḍilya from Kaiśorya Kāpya,
Kaiśorya Kāpya from Kumārahārita,
Kumārahārita from Gālava,
Gālava from Vidarbhīkauṇḍinya,
Vidarbhīkauṇḍinya from Vatsanapād Bābhrava,
Vatsanapād Bābhrava from Panthāḥ Saubhara,
Panthāḥ Saubhara from Ayāsya Āṅgirasa,
Ayāsya Āṅgirasa from Ābhūti Tvāṣṭra,
Ābhūti Tvāṣṭra from Viśvarūpa Tvāṣṭra,
Viśvarūpa Tvāṣṭra from the two Aśvins,
the two Aśvins from Dadhyañc Ātharvaṇa,

Dadhyañc Ātharvaṇa from Atharvan Daiva,
Atharvan Daiva from Mṛtyu Prādhvaṃsana,
Mṛtyu Prādhvaṃsana from Prādhvaṃsana,
Prādhvaṃsana from Ekarṣi,
Ekarṣi from Vipracitti,
Vipracitti from Vyaṣṭi,
Vyaṣṭi from Sanāru,
Sanāru from Sanātana,
Sanātana from Sanaga,
Sanaga from Parameṣṭin,
Parameṣṭin from *brahma*.[65]
brahma is the Self-existent. Adoration to *brahma*!

Here ends the sixth *Brāhmaṇa* of the fourth *Adhyāya*
Here ends the fourth *Adhyāya*

---

[65] Some commentators interpret this *brahma* as the creator god Brahmā. See fn under BU 1.3.21.

Fifth *Adhyāya*

First *Brāhmaṇa*

Fullness and The Implicate Order

That[1] is whole.[2] This is whole.
From wholeness, wholeness unfolds.[3]
Taking wholeness from wholeness,
wholeness remains.[4]

---

[1] Two pronouns are used here, *adas* and *idam* (see BU 2.3.1 fn). *Adas* is the "that" over there, and *idam* is the "this" directly before us. The "that" over there is *brahma,* the "this" before us is the world, and, because the "this" unfolds from the "that," it suggests that the "this" is a part of the "that." Therefore, this verse suggests a relationship between the whole and its parts. Yet there is a contradiction: Both are described as "wholes." In regular understanding, if a part is taken from a whole, the whole ceases to be complete and neither is the part. But in this way of seeing reality, the whole remains whole and even the part is whole—which suggests that within the part the whole exists and within the whole the part exists.

[2] Here the word is *pūrṇa*, which has been rendered as "whole," but it could also be taken as "complete" or "full."

[3] Here the verb is *udācyate,* comprised of *ut+ añc*. *Añc* means to bend or curl, *ut* is up; thus ut+*añc* is to bend or curl up, i.e., enfold. This suggests that one fullness is folded within another fullness. Some translators have taken *udācyate* as "arises."

[4] This verse is repeated verbatim in the IU invocation. There is a slightly modified version in AV 10.8.29.

Truly,[5] *brahma* is like the sky:[6] It is primal;[7] it is all-pervading.[8]

This wisdom was first spoken by the son of Kauravyayani. It is the knowledge of a *brahma*-knower. It is what truly needs to be known, and now I know it!

Here ends the first *Brāhmaṇa* of the fifth *Adhyāya*

Second *Brāhmaṇa*

Da Da Da!

1. The three sons of Prajapati, the gods, humans and demons,[9] all lived the life of a sacred student with their father. Having

---

[5] The word is *om,* and here it has been translated as a *maṅgala*, an auspicious invocation, "Truly!" However, it could also be rendered as a noun, in which case the sentence could read "The sound Om is *brahma*. It is like the sky..."

[6] The word is *kha*, which means the heavens or sky. Some translators have rendered it as ether.

[7] The word is *purāṇa.* Its meanings include old, ancient, and primal.

[8] The word is *vāyura,* literally "blowing like the wind," "windy." The sentence literally reads, "Space is windy."

[9] Here the words are *devas*, *manuṣyas* and *asuras*, gods, humans and demons. This could also be understood as different grades of humans, godly humans, regular humans and evil humans. Godly humans: those possessed of good qualities. Regular humans: those tending to be greedy. Evil humans: those possessed of a cruel nature. The point is different instructions are given to different natures of beings.

[10] Prajapati asked the demons to show kindness and compassion, for their nature is to be cruel and harmful.

lived as sacred students, the gods spoke to their father, "Good sir, teach us."

To the gods Prajapati uttered the syllable *da,* and then asked them, "Have you understood?"

The gods replied, "Yes, we have understood. You have instructed us: 'Show restraint (*dāmyata*)!'"

"Yes," he said, "you have understood."

2. Then the humans spoke to their father, "Good sir, teach us."

Prajapati uttered the syllable *da,* and then asked them, "Have you understood?"

They replied, "Yes, we have understood. You have instructed us: 'Give charity (*datta*)!'"

"Yes," he said, "you have understood."

3. Then the demons spoke to their father, "Good sir, teach us."

Prajapati uttered the syllable *da,* and then asked them, "Have you understood?"

They replied, "Yes, we have understood. You have instructed us: 'Show compassion (*dayadhvam*)!'"[10]

"Yes," he said, "you have understood."

Thunder, that divine voice in the sky, booms, "Da! Da! Da!" Thus these three, restraint, charity, and compassion, have been taught.

Here ends the second *Brāhmaṇa* of the fifth *Adhyāya*

---

[11] The word *hṛdaya* means "heart."

[12] Here *hṛ* is a verbal base which means either "to take away" or "to bring," depending on the context. The use of the pronoun "to him" (*asmai*) suggests the meaning "to bring" in this case.

[13] Here *da* means the verb *dā*, "to give."

[14] Here *ya* means the verb *yā*, "to go."

[15] Here there are two pronouns, *tad*, "that," and *etat*, "this." I take the "that" to be *brahma* and the "this" to be everything else, i.e., this world. Originally this world came from the "that," *brahma*, which is why the past tense is used.

[16] Here the expression is *mahad-yakṣa. Mahat* is great, and although a *yakṣa* is a particular kind of spirit, I have taken the word in a more general sense.

[17] The word is *satyam*. In later Sanskrit this word is commonly translated as "truth." Literally, *satya* is *sat-ya,* which means *sat*-ness. *Ya* is an abstract suffix. *Sat* means what is real, tangible and true. Therefore anything that is real, tangible and true can be called *satya*. See fn under BU 1.6.3 and 2.3.1. In this context "truth" does not fit the context. So I have rendered *satyam* as "creation" because the world around us is real, tangible and true.

Third *Brāhmaṇa*

The Heart

Hṛdaya, the heart,[11] is Prajapati, the Lord of Creation. It is *brahma*. It is all. It is formed of three syllables, *hṛ-da-ya*. The first syllable, *hṛ*, stands for "bringing," and so for one who understands *brahma,* people bring him what he needs.[12] The second syllable, *da*, stands for "giving," and so for one who understands *brahma,* people give him what he wants.[13] The third syllable, *ya*, stands for "going," and so for one who understands *brahma,* he goes to the heavenly worlds.[14]

Here ends the third *Brāhmaṇa* of the fifth *Adhyāya*

Fourth *Brāhmaṇa*

The Real

1. That is that and this was that,[15] namely, the Real. And one who knows this primordial great spirit[16] as the Real, as *brahma,* rules these worlds and overcomes what is unreal. Verily, the Real alone is *brahma;* the Real alone is *brahma!*

Here ends the fourth *Brāhmaṇa* of the fifth *Adhyāya*

Fifth *Brāhmaṇa*

Creation

1. In the beginning there was only water. Waters gave forth to creation.[17] Creation is *brahma*. *Brahma* gave forth to the lord

[18] In this early Upanishad this physical world is always viewed as real and not illusory. The view of the world as an illusion, as *māyā*, is an idea that came later in Hindu thought.
[19] Without *asat* there could be no *sat,* just as without down there could be no up. Therefore, *asat* is necessary. Creation cannot exist without duality.
[20] Here the morphology of the word *satya* is different. Instead of being divided into two parts, it has been divided into three syllables, *sa-ti-ya,* where the first and last syllables indicate *sat* and the middle syllable indicates *asat*. This means that creation is comprised of three parts: two parts of *sat* and one part of *asat*. So *asat* is a part of creation, but only a one-third portion. Here it is said that in spite of knowing this, a person who still focuses on the *asat* is ultimately lost. In the mythology of the later tradition an *asura* embraces the *asat* side of life while the *suras* embrace the *sat* side. This is why good always triumphs over evil, because two-thirds of creation is *sat* while only one-third is *asat*.
[21] The relationship between the universe and the human body is a recurrent theme throughout the Upanishads and the later Hindu tradition. There has been reference to the sun and the right eye already. See BU 2.3.4. These ideas are based on the idea mentioned in BU 5.1 that there is a relationship between the whole and the parts. This also ties into the Rig Veda idea of the universe being the cosmic body of God. See RV 10.90 (*Puruṣa Sukta*), where the sun is said to be the eye of that Great Being, the wind the breathing of that Great Being, the moon the mind of that great being, and so forth.
[22] The word is *prāṇa.*
[23] The Sanskrit is *utkramisyan*, which is literally "stepping out." When the soul "steps away" from the body, it is called death.
[24] *Bhūr*, *bhuva* and *svar* are called the *mahāvyāhṛti,* "the great utterance," and it refers to the three regions, earth, sky and space, or, in more general terms, the lower, middle, and (continued page 159)

of creatures, Prajapati. The lord of creatures gave forth to the gods, who in turn, revered this creation as real (*satya*).[18] *Satya* is made of three syllables, *sa*, *ti*, and *ya*. The first and the last syllables indicate *sat*, what is real, while the middle syllable, *ti*, indicates *asat,* what is unreal.[19] This unreal is held between the real. Therefore the real always exists. One who knows this is never harmed by the unreal.[20]

2. That yonder sun is real. The person in the orb of the sun and the person in the right eye depend on each other.[21] The person in the orb of the sun connects to the person in the right eye through its rays, while the person in the right eye connects to the person in the orb of the sun through its vital breaths.[22] At the time of death[23] one is able to clearly see this orb because those rays no longer touch him.

3. *Bhūr* is the head of this person in the sun disk.[24] There is one head, so there is one syllable. *Bhuva* is his arms. There are two arms, so there are two syllables. *Svar* (*su*+ *ar*) is his feet. There are two feet, so there are two syllables. His secret name is *ahar*, the day. One who knows this vanquishes evil and leaves it behind.

4. *Bhūr* is the head of this person in the right eye. There is one head, so there is one syllable. *Bhuva* is his arms. There are two arms, so there are two syllables. *Svar* is his feet. There are two feet, so there are two syllables. His secret name is *aham*, I. One who knows this vanquishes evil and leaves it behind.

Here ends the fifth *Brāhmaṇa* of the fifth *Adhyāya*

Sixth *Brāhmaṇa*

The Lord in the Heart

1. Being the size of a grain of rice, this person, consisting of mind, is situated within the heart and shines forth.[25] He is the lord, he is the ruler, and he governs all things of this realm.

Here ends the sixth *Brāhmaṇa* of the fifth *Adhyāya*

Seventh *Brāhmaṇa*

Brahma as lightning

"*Brahma* is lightning!" Lightning pierces and cuts darkness. So one who knows *brahma* as lightning is cut away from all evil. Indeed, *brahma* is lightning.[26]

---

upper regions. What is notable here is the reversal of order. In the later tradition *bhūr* is the terrestrial region associated with the feet of the cosmic body while *svar* is the highest region, the heavens, and is associated with the head of the cosmic body. Yet here in this early tradition, the order is reversed. I suspect the reason for this is because the world within and the world without, the microcosm and the macrocosm, were seen as reflections of each other. So what would be viewed as up at this level would be seen as down at that level.

[25] In the later tradition this theme has been further developed. Whole descriptions of this Lord within the heart can be found. In the Bhagavat Purana (2.2.8). For example, this person has been described as *paramātmā*, God within the heart, and is said to be the size of a *prādeśa*, the span of the thumb to the forefinger.

[26] For another description of *brahma* and lightning see Kena 4.4.

Here ends the seventh *Brāhmaṇa* of the fifth *Adhyāya*

Eighth *Brāhmaṇa*

Speech and the Milk Cow

Speech is compared to a milk-cow with four nipples, *svāhā, vaṣaṭ, hanta,* and *svadhā.* The gods exist on two nipples, *svāhā* and *vaṣaṭ.* Human beings exist on *hanta,* and the ancestors exist on *svadhā.* The bull of this cow is the life airs and her calf is the mind.

Here ends the eighth *Brāhmaṇa* of the fifth *Adhyāya*

Ninth *Brāhmaṇa*

The Universal Fire Within

1. There is a universal fire within a person by which he both cooks and digests his food. The roar of this fire can be heard when one covers the ears. However, at the time of death, when one leaves this body, this sound can no longer be heard.

Here ends the ninth *Brāhmaṇa* of the fifth *Adhyāya*

Tenth *Brāhmaṇa*

Leaving this world

1. When a person passes from this world he reaches the wind. There a hole the size of a chariot wheel opens by which he reaches a higher level. He then reaches the sun. Thereupon a

hole the size of a drum opens by which he reaches a still higher level. He then reaches the moon. Upon reaching the moon a hole the size of a kettle drum opens by which he reaches an even higher level. Finally, he reaches a world without suffering where he dwells for eternity.

Here ends the tenth *Brāhmaṇa* of the fifth *Adhyāya*

Eleventh *Brāhmaṇa*

The Sadness of Mortal Life

1. To suffer a disease is a great sadness. One who understands this attains the supreme destination. To take a departed one to

---

[27] The experience and realization of death leads to the questioning of life, which in turn leads to striving to overcome death. Ultimately this leads to *brahma*.

[28] The two words used here are *anna* and *prāṇa*, food and life force. *Prāṇa* could also be taken as breath.

[29] Commentators suggest that the syllable *vi* is the verbal base *viś*, which means "to enter." Beings "enter" into food when they enter this world. The theme of food is prominent throughout the Upanishads.

[30] Commentators suggest that the syllable *ram* is the verbal base, which means "to rejoice." To live, to breathe, to consume food, to procreate, are enjoyable.

[31] The two syllables *"vi" and "ram"* suggest the two driving forces of this world, i.e., food and pleasure. All beings in this world are driven to seek these two elements. Yet there is another meaning. Together these two syllables form the word *virāma,* which means to stop. The suggestion is to resist the drives of this world. Thus the theme of renunciation is indicated.

the wilderness for cremation is a great sadness. One who understands this attains the supreme destination. To lay a departed one onto the funeral pyre is a great sadness. One who understands this attains the supreme destination.[27]

Here ends the eleventh *Brāhmaṇa* of the fifth *Adhyāya*

Twelfth *Brāhmaṇa*

Food and Life Force

1. It has been said "Food is *brahma*." But this is not true. Without life energy, food spoils. Therefore it has been said "Life energy is *brahma*."[28] But this is also not true because without food life energy withers away. It is only when these two gods become one that they become important.

In this regard Pradrida asked his father, "Is there any benefit for one who knows this?"

With the wave of his hand, his father said, "None, Pradrida. No one attains the supreme just by knowing the union of these two. But consider this: "*vi*" is food because all beings are built on food;[29] "*ram*" is life energy because all beings rejoice in life energy.[30] All beings celebrate one who understands this.[31]

Here ends the twelfth *Brāhmaṇa* of the fifth *Adhyāya*

Thirteenth *Brāhmaṇa*

Uktha, Yajus, Sāman, Kṣatra as Life Force[32]

1. One should consider life force as *uktha,* support. All things are supported and lifted up by life force. One who knows this

---

[32] In this chapter four elements are raised: *uktha*, *yajus*, *sāman* and *kṣatra*. *Uktha* is derived from *vac*, speech, and it means that human speech and language arise from life force. *Yajus* is derived from *yuj,* to be in union, and it means that inherent in life force is the ability to unify. *Sāman* is derived from *śam*, to pacify and find peace, that life force gives rise to peace; and *kṣatra* is derived from *kṣin*, to have dominion, that life force gives rise to order and governance. Many traditional commentators associate these four words with the four Vedas, Rig, Yajur, Sāma and Atharva. I have not followed this approach in these translations.

[33] This chapter is a commentary on *gāyatrī.* Strictly speaking *gāyatrī* is the name of a meter in Sanskrit with twenty-four syllables arranged in three lines. Therefore, there are eight beats in each line. A line is called a *pada,* and usually a verse has four *padas* or feet. In the case of the *gāyatrī* meter there are only three *padas*. What is commonly understood as *gāyatrī,* however, is a specific mantra from the Rig Veda (3.62.10) addressed to Savitri, the sun. This verse is also in *gāyatrī* meter, three lines of eight beats per *pada*.

tat savitur vareṇyaṃ,
bhargo devasya dhimahi,
dhiyo yo naḥ pracodayāt

[34] These three words respectively mean the earth, sky, and the heavens. They are analogous to *bhur, bhuvas, suvaḥ*.

stands mighty and resides intimately with *uktha*.

2. One should consider life force as *yajus,* unification. All beings are unified by life force, and for one who knows this all beings come together for his supremacy and he resides intimately with *yajus*.

3. One should consider life force as *sāman,* balance. All beings are balanced by life force, and for one who knows this all beings come together for his supremacy and he resides intimately with *sāman*.

4. One should consider life force as *kṣatra,* power. Life force protects one from harm, and one who has achieved this power needs no protection. One who understands this becomes intimate with and resides intimately with *kṣatra*.

Here ends the thirteenth *Brāhmaṇa* of the fifth *Adhyāya*

Fourteenth *Brāhmaṇa*

Gāyatrī[33]

1. *Bhūmi, antarikṣa* and *dyau*[34] are eight syllables that together make the first line of a *gāyatrī verse.* This line is the same as these three words. To the extent one understands this first line, one is endowed with land that extends as far as these three worlds.

2. *Ṛcah, yajūṃṣi* and *sāmānī*[35] are eight syllables that together make another line of a *gāyatrī* verse. This second line is the same as the three words in the first line: eight beats. To the extent one understands this second line, one is endowed with knowledge.

---

[35] These three words are the plural forms of the names of the three Vedas, Rig, Yajur and Sama Vedas. The Vedas constitute knowledge.

[36] These are the three "breaths," the incoming breath, the outgoing breath and the held-breath, respectively. For an earlier reference see BU 3.9.4 and 3.9.25, and CU 1.3.7.

[37] *Parorajas* is literally *paras-rajas*. *Paras* means "beyond" or "in the distance." *Rajas* can be "sky," "dust," or even "gloom." It can also suggest "burning" and "shining." So *parorajas* is open to numerous interpretations. Here it has been taken as that which shines up above or in the distance, i.e., the sun, but it could also be "the one who shines above the gloom." Some gloss it as "the super-mundane." The meaning is *brahma*.

[38] This suggests "might is right."

[39] The word is *adhyātmā.* See BU 3.7.16. Here, as in many other places, the meaning is contextual. Here the context is physical strength *(bala)* and life breaths *(prāṇa),* so we have chosen to take *ātmā* as "the body." *Adhi,* as a prefix, means "in relation to." So *adhyātmā* is "relating to the body" or "within the body."

[40] The Sanskrit word is *gaya.* Literally, *gaya* is one's family or house guests, but it is also wealth. So here the body is the house and the *prāṇas* are the family or guests who reside within.

3. *Prāṇa*, *apānā* and *vyāna*[36] are eight syllables that together make the third line of a *gāyatrī* verse. This third line is the same as the three words in the first and second lines: eight beats each. To the extent one understands this third line, one is endowed with life force.

And then there is a fourth (*turīya*), most wonderful *(darśatam)* hidden line of *gāyatrī* that points to that shining One beyond this world *(parorajā)*.[37] *Turīya* means "fourth." *Darśatam* means "visible." *Parorajā* means "shining beyond." To the extent one understands this fourth and hidden line of *gāyatrī,* one shines with fame and glory.

4. This *gāyatrī* is founded on that One who shines beyond this world. It is founded on truth, and truth is something seen. Therefore, seeing is truth. If two people are quarreling and one says, "I saw it," and the other says, "I heard it," we have the most confidence in the one who said, "I saw it."

And truth in turn is founded on strength, *bala*. Strength indeed is life force because it is founded on breath. Therefore they say "strength is more powerful than even truth."[38] In this way *gāyatrī* is established from within the body[39] and it protects one's wealth.[40] One's wealth is the bodily senses, so *gāyatrī* protects the senses. And because it protects this wealth, it is called *gāyatrī*. It is the same as that *sāvitrī gāyatrī* which is commonly recited. And so it protects the life breath of anyone who recites this *gāyatrī.*

5. Some recite a *sāvitṛī gāyatrī* that is in *anuṣṭubh meter*[41] as the real *gāyatrī,* saying speech in general is *anuṣṭubh,*[42] but this is not correct. One should recite the *savitṛī gāyatrī*[43] that is in *gāyatrī* meter. But even if one recites this *anuṣṭubh gāyatrī* and receives a good reward, it does not equal even a single line of the real *gāyatrī.*

6. On the other hand, if one should receive all the wealth of

---

[41] Like *gāyatrī, anuṣṭubh* is a type of meter in Sanskrit prosody consisting of four lines of eight syllables, making a total of thirty-two syllables. It is the most common meter in Sanskrit. Most of the Ramayana, the Mahabharata and the Puranas are in *anuṣṭubh* meter.

Some commentators suggest the following hymn as the *anuṣṭubh gāyatrī* in question:

tat savitur vṛṇīmahe
vayaṃ devasya bhojanam
śreṣṭhaṃ sarva-dhātamam
turaṃ bhagasya dhīmahi RV (5.82.1)

The mantra is also quoted in CU 5.2.7.

[42] Apart from being the name of a meter *anuṣṭubh* simply means "speaking out."

[43] Here the reference is to the more common three line *gāyatrī* (RV 3.62.10).

tat savitur vareṇyaṃ
bhargo devasya dhīmahi
dhíyo yo naḥ prachodayāt

worlds, it would only equal the value of that first line of *gāyatrī.* If one should receive all the knowledge of the Vedas, it would only be the value of this second line of *gāyatrī.* If one should receive all the breath in this world, it would only be the value of this third line of *gāyatrī.* And then there is that fourth line, which is most wonderful and shines beyond this world. Hardly any person can attain this One. From where could one obtain anything more?

7. Here is the veneration of *gāyatrī*:

You are one-footed, O Gāyatrī.
You are two-footed.
You are three-footed, and you are four-footed.
But you are also without feet! For you never travel about.
Respects to your fourth line, the most wonderful of all,
As it refers to the One who shines above this world.

One full of malice, may he not attain good, may his desires never be fulfilled. In spite of knowing this *gāyatrī*, let that one who is full of malice never obtain his desires. Instead, may I obtain what he desires.

8. On this subject Janaka, King of Videha, spoke to Budila, the son of Ashvatarasha, "Did you not say you were a knower of *gāyatrī*? So how is it you have become a mere elephant, as it were, just carrying loads?"

Budila replied, "But, Your Majesty, I did not know its mouth."[44]

Janaka said, "Fire is its mouth! No matter how much fuel is laid

---

[44] The implied meaning is that because Budila's understanding was not complete, he was "burned" by the fire of this knowledge. In other words, his knowledge was incomplete. One commentator (Madhva) suggests that a *brāhmaṇa* who has this knowledge, yet still accepts priestly gifts from a benefactor, is just a beast of burden. One who has this knowledge no longer is dependent on any form of worldly support.

[45] *Brahmaṇa* 15 is repeated in IU 15-18.

[46] "O Sustainer of the Universe" is a translation of Pushan, a Vedic deity identified with the sun and, therefore, the surveyor of all things. This deity is also the conductor on journeys to the next world.

[47] "Glowing radiance" (*hiraṇmayena pātreṇa*) is literally "by a golden vessel." Some commentators interpret this as the sun.

[48] These verses are to be recited at the time of death or during a funeral ceremony. They reappear later, in IU 15-18.

[49] "O Creative Principal" is literally "descendent of Prajapati" (*prājāpatya*).

[50] "That most distant person of which I am a part" (*yo 'sāv asau puruṣaḥ so 'ham asmi*) is literally "that yonder person, he I am."'

[51] "O Supreme" is a gloss on *om*.

[52] "O Guiding Intelligence" and "O Grand Design" are both translations of "*kratu*," which is literally plan, design, intelligence, enlightenment, etc.

[53] Agni is the fire deity and, since the body is cremated, the prayer is to God as fire.

[54] "Forgive my sins" (*yuyodhy asmaj juhurāṇam*) is literally "overcome" or "battle our crooked ways."

on a fire, it consumes everything. Similarly, for one who has this knowledge, no matter how much evil is done, it is consumed by the fire of this knowledge, and that person becomes clean and pure, ageless and immortal.

Here ends the fourteenth *Brāhmaṇa* of the fifth *Adhyāya*

Fifteenth *Brāhmaṇa*

Prayer of the Dying[45]

O Sustainer of the Universe,[46] your glowing radiance[47] covers your face of truth. O God of light, I am a lover of truth. I wish to see you now. Please reveal yourself.[48]

O Sustainer, Sole Seer, Controller, O Sun, O Creative Principle,[49] diffuse your glaring radiance, focus your light. I wish to behold your most wonderful form, that most distant person of which I am a part.[50]

O Supreme,[51] my breath to the immortal wind, this body to ashes. O Guiding Intelligence, remember all that I have done. O Grand Design,[52] remember my deeds. Do not forget me.

O Agni,[53] lead me to prosperity. O God, you alone know the way. Vanquish my sins.[54] To you I offer unlimited prayer.

Here ends the fifteenth *Brāhmaṇa* of the fifth *Adhyāya*

Here ends the fifth *Adhyāya*

Sixth *Adhyāya*

First *Brāhmaṇa*

Breath: The Oldest and the Greatest[1]

1. One who knows the oldest[2] and the greatest becomes the oldest and the greatest. Breath is the oldest and the greatest! And one who knows this becomes the oldest and the greatest within his own circle and amongst all others whom he desires.

2. One who knows the most excellent becomes the most excellent. Speech is the most excellent! And one who knows this becomes the most excellent within his own group and amongst all others whom he desires.

3. For one who knows the foundation, he has a foundation on both even and uneven ground. Sight is the foundation, for with the eye one has a foundation. One who knows this always has a foundation on both even and uneven ground.

4. For one who knows wealth, wealth comes to him and his desires are fulfilled. Hearing is wealth, for with the ear all the Vedas are known. For one who knows this, wealth comes to him and his desires are fulfilled.

---

[1] See CU 5.1 and KauU 3.3 for similar descriptions.

[2] Breath begins to function within an embryo before the other functions; therefore, breath is declared to be the eldest.

5. One who knows the resting place becomes the resting place for his own kinsmen and for the common man. The mind indeed is the resting place. One who knows this becomes the resting place for his own kinsmen and for people in general.

6. One who knows procreation is blessed with offspring and cattle. Semen is procreation. One who knows this is blessed with offspring and cattle.

7. The vital functions once quarreled over who was the best, so they went to Prajapati[3] and asked, "Who amongst us is superior?"

Prajapati replied, "Let each of you step away from the body. The one whose absence makes the body the worst is superior."

8. Speech left first. He remained away for a year and then returned and asked, "How were you able to live without me?"

"We lived without speaking, as the dumb; but we breathed with breath, we saw with the eye, we heard with the ear, we thought with the mind, and we procreated with semen. In this way we lived." Speech re-entered.

9, Then sight left. He remained away for a year and then returned and asked, "How were you able to live without me?"

---

[3] The word here is *brahma,* which is here glossed as Prajapati, the Vedic deity of creation.

"We lived without seeing, as the blind; but we breathed with breath, we spoke with speech, we heard with the ear, we thought with the mind, and we procreated with semen. In this way we lived." Sight re-entered.

10. Then hearing left. He remained away for a year and then returned and asked, "How were you able to live without me?"

"We lived without hearing, as the deaf; but we breathed with breath, we spoke with speech, we saw with the eye, we thought with the mind, and we procreated with semen. In this way we lived." Hearing re-entered.

11. Then the mind left. He remained away for a year and then returned and asked, "How were you able to live without me?"

"We lived without thinking, as an idiot; but we breathed with breath, we spoke with speech, we saw with the eye, we heard with the ear, and we procreated with semen. In this way we lived." The mind re-entered.

12. Then semen left. He remained away for a year and then returned and asked, "How were you able to live without me?"

"We lived without procreating, as the impotent would; but we breathed with breath, we spoke with speech, we saw with the eye, we heard with the ear, and we thought with the mind. In this way we lived." Semen re-entered.

13. Then breath began to leave and uproot all the others. As a great stallion[4] kicks up its tethers, all the vital functions cried out, "Lord, don't leave! Without you we will not be able to live!"

"Then make me some tribute!" breath demanded.

"Yes, anything!"

14. Then speech said, "I was the most excellent; now you are the most excellent." The eye said, "I was the foundation; now you are the foundation." The ear said, "I was wealth; now you are wealth." The mind said, "I was the resting place, now you are the resting place." Semen said, "I was procreation; now you are procreation."

Breath then asked, "So what will be my food and what will be my clothing?[5]

---

[4] Here the horse is mentioned as a *mahā-suhayaḥ saindhavaḥ*, a great-spirited stallion of the Sindh region.

[5] The Sanskrit word is *vāsa*, which has many meanings, including clothing and residence. Many commentators take this as residence.

[6] Jaivali Pravahana is the philosopher King of Panchala who appears in both the Brihad Aranyaka Upanishad (6.2.1) and the Chandogya Upanishad (5.4.8). He is a contemporary of King Janaka of Videha and is among the most famous kings of Uttara Pañchāla-ratha. He teaches Shvetaketu, son of Uddalaka Aruni. His assembly was where the elites of society would meet to discuss the issues of the day.

[7] This is the first of five questions Jaivali asks Shvetaketu.

They answered, "Everything in this world is your food, even down to the dog, the worm, and crawling and flying insects. Water is your clothing. Indeed, for one who knows that breath is food, there is nothing that cannot be eaten or accepted as food. Therefore, the wise who have learned the Vedas sip water before and after they eat. In this way they keep breath clothed."

Here ends the first *Brāhmaṇa* of the sixth *Adhyāya*

Second *Brāhmaṇa*
Life after Death

1. Once Shvetaketu, son of Aruni, went to the assembly of the Pañcālas and approached Jaivali Pravahana,[6] who was sitting in court. Seeing the boy, Jaivali addressed him, "Son!"

"Yes, sir?" replied Shvetaketu.

"Have you been instructed by your father?"

"Yes, sir." replied Shvetaketu.

2. "Do you know how beings depart this world and go to different locations?"[7]

"No, sir," replied Shvetaketu.

"Do you know how they return to this world?"

"No, sir," replied Shvetaketu.

"Do you know how the world beyond does not fill up in spite of so many beings continually going there?"

"No, sir," replied Shvetaketu.

"Do you know the ritual wherein water rises up and becomes a human voice and speaks?"

"No, sir, I do not," replied Shvetaketu.

"Do you know the path that leads to the gods? Do you know the path that leads to the ancestors? People who know this can go to the gods or the ancestors." In this regard there is the following saying:

"'Amongst mortals there are two paths:
The path to the gods, and the path to the forefathers.
All beings travel between these two:
Mother earth and father heaven.'"

---

[8] The literal expression is *rājanya-bandhu*, friend of a king. It is a pejorative expression.

[9] In this version of the story Shvetaketu is portrayed as a brat. In the CU version of the story his demeanor has been improved.

[10] This is the *gotra* (paternal lineage) name for the father. His actual name was Uddalaka Aruni.

Shvetaketu replied, "Sir, I do not know the answer to any of these questions."

3. With that Jaivali invited the boy to stay and learn, but the boy rejected the invitation and ran home to his father. At home he said to his father, "Good sir! You have always said that I am educated! This is a farce!"

"How so, my intelligent boy?" replied his father.

"This excuse for a king[8] put five questions before me and I did not know the answer to a single one!"

"What were the questions?" asked his father.

"These," and the boy repeated the questions.

4. His father replied, "You know me, my son. Whatever I know I have taught you. Come, let us go to Jaivali and live as students and learn."

The boy replied, "You go alone, sir."[9]

So Shvetaketu's father, Gautama,[10] went to Jaivali Pravahana on his own, wherein he was greeted with a respectful seat and proper refreshments.

Jaivali Pravahana then declared, "Let us give you a boon. Ask what you wish, O Gautama."

5. Gautama replied, "Now that you have given me this boon, please tell me the answers to the questions you have asked my son."

6. "Gautama," Jaivali replied, "these are matters of the gods. Please ask things which are more human in nature."

7. Gautama said, "It is well known that I have my share of gold, cows, horses, servant girls, followers and apparels. Good sir, do not place limits on what is abundant, infinite and unlimited."

"Then desire it in the proper way!" replied Jaivali.[11]

---

[11] In other words, Jaivali asked Gautama to formally declare himself to be a student. By caste, Gautama, being a *brāhmana*, was in a higher position than Jaibali, who was a *kṣatriya*. Therefore, Gautama would not ordinarily submit to Jaivali for instruction. This is why his son was so indignant to return for instruction. Yet, for the sake of obtaining this knowledge, Gautama willingly became Jaivali's student.

[12] Since Gautama was of a higher caste than the king, he was allowed to become a student of the king without having to perform the usual menial service, including touching the feet of the king. Instead, all he had to do was declare himself a student and that would suffice.

[13] In those days knowledge was not universally disseminated, but was held in tight family and teacher-student groups.

[14] This is the beginning of the doctrine of the five fires, *pancha-agni vidyā*. It is taught here as well as in the CU 5.3.10. The heavens, the sky (the clouds), the earth, man and woman are seen as altars of burning fire. In other words, the *yajña*, the sacrifice, is a metaphor for life. All life is a sacrificial fire that needs to be tended to.

"Good sir, I come to you as a student."

With such words, this is how it was done in the past. Gautama declared himself a student and lived with Jaivali Pravahana.[12]

8. Jaivali then spoke. "Gautama, since this knowledge has never resided with any priestly family before,[13] neither you nor your ancestors should take offense with me. I will gladly teach you this knowledge. How can I refuse when you are speaking in this respectful manner?"

9. Jaivali continued, "Gautama, the worlds up there, the heavens, are a sacrificial fire![14] The sun is its fuel. The sun's rays are its smoke. The day is its flame. The directions are its burning coals. Its intermediate directions are the sparks. Into this fire the gods pour faith, and King Soma, the moon, arises from this sacrifice.

10. "Gautama, a rain cloud is a sacrificial fire! The year is its fuel. The clouds are its smoke. Lightning is its flame. Thunder is its coals and hail the sparks. Into this fire the gods offer King Soma, and from that fire come rains.

11. "Gautama, this world here is a sacrificial fire! The earth is its fuel. Fire is its smoke. The night is its flame. The moon is its coals and the lunar mansions its sparks. Into this fire the gods offer rains, and from that fire comes food.

12. "Gautama, a man is a sacrificial fire! His open mouth is its

fuel. Breath is its smoke. Speech is its flame. His eyes are its coals and his ears its sparks. Into this fire the gods offer food, and from that fire semen arises.

13. "Gautama, a woman is a sacrificial fire! Her mid region is its fuel. Her bodily hair is its smoke. Her vagina is its flame. The act of entering her is its coals and her pleasure its sparks. Into this fire the gods pour semen, and from that fire a child is born.[15] He lives as long as he lives and then he dies.

14. "After he dies they offer him to the fire. In this case, the fire is the fire, the smoke is the smoke, the flame is the flame, the

---

[15] This is the answer to the fourth question: "Do you know the ritual wherein water rises up and becomes a human voice and speaks?"

[16] Literally, the color of light. This is perhaps a reference to the astral body.

[17] This could refer to householders, who live within society, or renunciants, who live outside of society, and how both are eligible to benefit from this knowledge. It could, however, refer to certain esoteric and secret doctrines that were practiced in the wilderness, away from society, by householders.

[18] Two paths to leave this world are mentioned here, the path of light and the path of darkness. A similar reference is made in BG 8.23-27.

[19] This is a reference to *uttarāyana*, the time between December 21st and June 21st, when the sun is on its northern path.

[20] For a parallel reference see CU 4.15.5.

[21] This is a reference to *dakṣināyana*, the time between June 21st and December 21st, when the sun is on its southern path.

[22] This refers to the waxing and waning of the moon.

coals are the coals, and the sparks are the sparks. Into this fire the gods offer this man, and from this offering the man emerges in radiant splendor.[16]

15. "Those who understand this and respect this truth with faith, whether they live here or in the wilderness,[17] enter the fire of cremation and follow the path of light.[18] From that flame they enter the day, and from the day they reach the waxing moon. From the waxing moon they attain the six months when the sun travels north,[19] and from there they reach the worlds of the gods. From the worlds of the gods they enter the sun, and from the sun they enter lightning. Finally, from lightning a person made of mind comes and directs them to the worlds of *brahma*. These exalted souls then dwell at a great distance and never return to this realm.[20]

16. "On the other hand, those who succeed in this world through sacrifice, charity and penance follow the path of darkness. They enter the smoke of the cremation fire and from there enter the night. From the night they attain the waning side of the moon, and from there they follow the six months when the sun moves towards the south.[21] After that they reach the realm of the ancestors. From the ancestors they attain the moon. Having attained the moon, they become food for the gods. There, as they are fed upon, the gods call out to King Soma, the moon, 'Increase! Decrease!'[22] After that they enter space and ultimately reach the wind, and from the wind they become rain and fall to the earth. Entering the earth, they once again become food and are offered into the fire of man. Finally, they are born in the fire

[23] This means they eventually lose the human form of life and gradually descend to lower species. This type of expression is common. See CU 5.10.7. There it is said such persons become dogs, swine or outcastes. There are many such references in the Upanishads and elsewhere.

[24] This chapter and the next one seem out of context, as if it were an afterthought added to the end of this Upanishad. Instead of *brahma*, *prana* and *ātmā*, and other lofty subjects, the subject matter of this chapter is procreation, women, babies and charms.

[25] The word for these preparatory rites is *upasat*. These include fasting, sipping water, touching the body with various gestures and prayers, etc.

[26] The sun appears to move in two directions along the eastern horizon according to the time of the year. From December to June it moves north (*uttarayāyana*), and from June to December it moves south (*dakṣināyana*). As the sun moves northward the days become longer and so there is more light in the world. As the sun moves southwards the days become shorter. Activities performed in light are always preferred.

[27] The lunar month is divided into two parts called *pakṣas* or wings, the waxing moon and the waning moon. Activities performed during the waxing fortnight, as the moon's light increases, are always more auspicious.

[28] In Vedic astronomy the 360 degrees of the solar ecliptic are divided into 27 segments of 13-1/3 degrees called *nakṣtras,* one for each day of the lunar month. Some of these *nakṣtras* are considered male, others female, and still others neuter.

[29] The word here is *mantha*. This mixture is created gradually as each offering is made into the fire. When each mantra is recited a certain amount of clarified butter (ghee) is added to the fire, after which a few remaining drops of ghee are left on the spoon which are successively added to a small bowl that is beside the fire on the edge of the fire pit. That left-over ghee constitutes the mixture.

of woman and once again appear in these worlds. In this way they continue to rotate in this world.

"These are the two paths, and those who do not understand this become insects, moths and snakes."[23]

Here ends the second *Brāhmaṇa* of the sixth *Adhyāya*

Third *Brāhmaṇa*

A Fire Ritual for Greatness[24]

1. If a man desires greatness, let him first perform the usual preparatory rites for twelve days.[25] This should be done at an auspicious time during the six months when the sun is traveling north[26] and during the time of the waxing moon.[27] Let him then bring together the necessary herbs, fruits, utensils and bowls. Let him sweep an area clean and purify it by smearing cow dung. Let him build a fire and purify the clarified butter in the proper manner. Then, on a day governed by a male lunar mansion,[28] let him offer oblations into the fire and create a mixture.[29]

The mantras:[30]

O Fire! To all those gods under your control, who can block the desires of man, I offer a share of this sacrifice. Let them be satisfied and let them satisfy all my desires.

And to that goddess who lays across my path as a stumbling block and thinks "I am the disposer," to you I offer this stream of butter as an appeasement.

2. He should then offer butter into the fire with the following prayers: "Hail to the eldest! Hail to the best!" A small portion is then added to the mixture. Here the offering is to the breath.

"Hail to the most excellent!" A small portion is then added to the mixture. Here the offering is to speech.

"Hail to the foundation!" A small portion is then added to the mixture. Here the offering is to the eye.

"Hail to wealth!" A small portion is then added to the mixture. Here the offering is to the ear.

"Hail to the resting place!" A small portion of ghee is then added to the mixture. Here the offering is to the mind.

"Hail to procreation!" A small portion is then added to the mixture. Here the offering is to semen.

---

[30] What follows is a series of mantras that are recited as offerings of clarified butter are offered into the fire. In some ways a translation of the mantras is unnecessary and even counterproductive. The point is the sound of the mantras and the mental intention behind those prayers.

[31] *Bhū bhuva svaḥ* are called the *vyahṛtis*, "the great utterance," and they are always recited during a fire ritual. They are also recited at the beginning of the *savitṛ gāyatrī.*

In this way, each time butter is offered into the fire a small portion is then added to the mixture.

3. Continuing, "Hail to fire!"

"Hail to Soma!"

"Hail to *bhū*!"

"Hail to *bhuva*!"

"Hail to *svah*!"

"Hail to *bhū, bhuva svah*!"[31]

"Hail to *brāhmaṇa*!"

"Hail to *kṣatra*!"

"Hail to *bhūta,* the past!"

"Hail to *bhaviṣya,* the future!"

"Hail to *viśva*, the universe!"

"Hail to *sarva*, the whole!"

"Hail to Prajapati, the Creator!"

4. Thereafter, touching the mixture, one should say, "You are always flowing (as breath), you are blazing (as fire), you are full (as the sky). You are steadfast (as the earth). You are the sole resort. You are the sound *hiṅ* made at the beginning of a sacrifice, and you are even the making of the sound *hiṅ*. You are the high chant[32] and you are the making of the high chant. You are the call out and the call back.[33] You are the flash in the cloud.[34] You are power. You are food. You are lighting. You are destruction, and you are the final absorption."

5. He then raises up the mixture and says, "You know your greatness and I know it too. You are the king, the controller and the overlord. Make me the king, the controller and the overlord."

6. He sips from the cup and again says,

"tat savitur vareṇyam

"Honey are the winds! Honey are the rivers!
Both envelop a righteous man.

---

[32] The high chant is a particular chant recited by all the priests at a certain point in a *yajña*. The volume becomes very loud. For a further reference see fn under BU 1.3.1.

[33] During a fire sacrifice there are often many priests. The call out is a chant that is recited by a priest or priests and the call back is the "echo" chant back by other priests.

[34] Literally, the flame in a cloud.

May plants and healing herbs be full of sweetness for us.
Bhūḥ svāhā

"bhargo devasya dhīmahi

"Honey is the night! Honey is the dawn! Honey is this earth. Honey is the sky, and honey are these heavens. May they become our father. *Bhuvaḥ svāḥā*

"dhiyo yo naḥ pracodayāt

"Honey-filled are trees. Honey-filled is the sun.
Honey-filled are cows. May they bless us! *svāḥā"*

Reciting this *sāvitṛ* hymn along with these honey prayers, let him say,

"May I become all this, the earth, the sky and the heavens. *svāḥā*!"

Finally, sipping water and washing his hands, let him lay down behind the fire with his head facing east and in the morning let him worship the fire and say, "You are the one lotus amongst all the directions. Let me become the one lotus amongst all men." Then let him sit and recite his family lineage.

7. In this manner Uddalaka Aruni explained this to his disciple Vajasaneya Yajnavalkya, and then said, "If one were to sprinkle this mixture on a dead and dried stump, it would sprout branches

and grow green leaves!"

8. Then Vajasaneya Yajnavalkya explained this to his disciple Madhuka Paingya and said, "If one were to sprinkle this mixture on a dead and dried stump, it would sprout branches and grow green leaves!"

9. Then Madhuka Paingya explained this to his disciple Cula Bhagavitti and said, "If one were to sprinkle this mixture on a dead and dried stump, it would sprout branches and grow green leaves!"

10. Then Cula Bhagavitti explained this to his disciple Janaki Ayasthuna and said, "If one were to sprinkle this mixture on a dead and dried stump, it would sprout branches and grow green leaves!"

11. Then Janaki Ayasthuna explained this to his disciple Satyakama Jabali and said, "If one were to sprinkle this mixture on a dead and dried stump, it would sprout branches and grow green leaves!"

---

[35] The word is *pratiṣṭhā,* which can also mean "resting place" or "home."

[36] Here the exact words are "*adha upāsta.*" *Adhas* is "down below," *upāsta* is "to attend to." Therefore, *adha upāsta* is literally "to attend to down below."

[37] Again, the Sanskrit is "to attend to her down below."

[38] Here the word is *grāvan,* which is a stone used in ritual like a pestle.

12. Then Satyakama Jabali explained this to his disciple and said, "If one were to sprinkle this mixture on a dead and dried stump, it would sprout branches and grow green leaves!"

One must not explain this to anyone who is not a son or disciple!

13. Four things are made of fig-wood: the sacrificial spoons, the bowls, the burning wood, and the two mixing sticks. There are ten varieties of cultivated grains to be used: rice, barley, sesame, bean, millet, wheat, lentil, pulse, pea, and legume. All these are to be ground and mixed with yogurt, honey, and clarified butter, and then offered into the fire with each sacrificial offering.

Here ends the third *Brāhmana* of the sixth *Adhyāya*

Fourth *Brāhmaṇa*

Procreation and Sacrifice

1. Of all creation, earth is the essence; and of the earth, water is the essence. Of water, herbs are the essence; and of herbs, flowers are the essence. Of flowers, fruits are the essence; and of all fruits, man is the essence. And of man, semen is his very essence.

2. And then the Lord of Creatures, Prajapati, thought, "Let me create a foundation[35] for this semen." So Prajapati created woman. Having created her, he impregnated her.[36] Therefore, a man should have intercourse with a woman.[37] He extended out from himself a hard part,[38] like the stone used to press *soma*,

which he used to impregnate her.

3. Indeed, her lap is a sacrificial altar. Her bodily hair is the sacred *kuśa* grass. The outer lips of her vagina are the two stones of the *soma* press. Her inner lips hold the fire within. A man who engages in sexual intercourse with a woman gains the same result as a man who performs the *soma* sacrifice.[39] A man who understands this and goes to a woman gains the merit of women; yet a man who does not know this and yet still goes to a woman loses his merit to her.

4-5. Knowing this, Uddaka Aruni, Naka Maudgalya and Kumara Harita have all said, "Many mortal men, even a *brāhmana*

---

[39] Here the exact word is *vājapeya*, which is one of the forms of the *soma* sacrifice.

[40] Here the expression "the fires and their altars" refers to the bodily functions. During sex these functions have been overly stimulated and need to return to their usual state.

[41] The implied meaning is if a man discharges semen in water, he may not be able to touch it, so he may simply address his reflection in water.

[42] The verb is *avakrī*, which means to buy off or bribe.

[43] This verse unfortunately condones violence towards women. It is misogynistic. A verse like this comes out of a different time and place and has to be seen in that context. Today such practices are unacceptable and must be rejected. This chapter and the previous one are believed to be an afterthought added to the end of this Upanishad. In fact, this section seems out of place with the general tenor of the BU, and in no other place within the principal Upanishads do we find this kind of comment.

by descent, have departed this world impotent and without merit, having engaged in sexual intercourse without this understanding."

If a man discharges semen in his sleep or while awake, whether a little or a lot, he must touch it and recite the following mantra:

"I reclaim whatever semen I have lost that may have fallen on the earth or vegetation or flowed into water. May I reclaim my virility, luster, and good fortune. May the fires and their altars be arranged in their usual place."[40]

He should then hold that semen between the thumb and the ring finger and rub it on his brow or chest.

6-7. Now, if he sees his reflection in water he must also recite: "May luster, vigor, fame, wealth, and merit always remain in me."[41]

A woman is most beautiful who has finished her period and removed her stained clothes. Such a woman should be approached and invited for intimacy. If she does not consent, she should be offered gifts.[42] If still she does not consent, she should be beaten with a stick or the hand, and the man should say, "I take away your splendor with my power and glory." In this way she is disgraced.[43]

8. If she consents the man should say, "With my power and glory I confer all splendor on you." In this way they both become glorious.

9. A man who desires a woman and so thinks, "She must love me," should kiss her and stroke her vagina and finally place his member in her while softly repeating,

"From my body you arose. From my heart you are born.
You are the very essence of my body. Make her mad with passion for me as if struck by Cupid's arrow."[44]

10. If he does not want her to conceive, upon placing his member in her, he must join his mouth to hers and breathe into her and then pull that breath back while thinking, "With power and virility I take back my semen. In this way she will not conceive."[45]

---

[44] Literally, the expression is "*digdha-viddhām iva,*" "as if pierced by an enchanted arrow."

[45] The words are *mukhena mukham sandhāya,* "placing the mouth on the mouth." The word *mukham* simply means an opening, which ordinarily means the opening of the face, but could also mean the opening of the vagina. Perhaps this suggests a form of birth control that involves sucking back semen.

[46] Normally the reeds of the *kuśa* grass are placed on the northern and southern sides of the sacrificial container with their tips facing to the east. "In the reverse order" means the reeds are placed with the tips facing west.

[47] Literally, it says *para*, "superior." The evoking of charms and spells was common during the time of the Upanishads. This whole chapter suggests a connection with the Atharva Veda, which is full of such charms and spells.

11. If, on the other hand, he wants her to conceive, upon placing his member in her and joining his mouth to hers, he should inhale and then breathe into her thinking, "With power and virility I place my seed in you." In this way she conceives.

12. Now, if the man's wife should have a lover whom he wishes to harm, he can perform the following charm. He should place fire into a greenware pot and arrange *kuśa* grass in the reverse order[46] and then offer them into the fire with the following prayers:

(Adding the person's name to the end of each prayer.)
You have sacrificed in my fire! I take from you your incoming and outgoing breaths.
You have sacrificed in my fire! I take from you your sons and livestock.
You have sacrificed in my fire! I take from you your sacrifices and merit.
You have sacrificed in my fire! I take from you your hopes and dreams.

A man cursed in this way by a learned *brāhmana* will leave this world senseless and devoid of merit. Therefore, one should not play with the wife of a *brāhmana* who knows this, for such a knowledgeable man is not to be trifled with.[47]

13. Now, when a man finds that his wife is having her period, for three days she must not drink from metal cups or wear new clothes. Neither should she be touched by a low caste man or

woman. But then, after three nights, she should bathe and resume her regular duties.[48]

14. Afterwards, if the man should desire a son with a fair complexion, who is learned in one Veda and who will have a long life, he should have his wife cook rice boiled in milk with clarified butter. Together they should then eat this and it will make them capable to have such a child.

15. If he should desire a son with a tawny complexion and brown eyes, who is learned in two Vedas and who will have a long life, he should have his wife cook rice made with yogurt and clarified butter. Together they should eat this and it will make them capable to have such a child.

16. If he should desire a son with a dark complexion and reddish

---

[48] Here the Sanskrit is literally "pound rice," *vrīhīn avaghātayet.*

[49] Many traditional commentators detract from a woman's right for learning sacred knowledge by stating that what is meant here is only learning in terms of domestic affairs (*gṛiha-tantra-viṣayam*).

[50] Here the words are *paṇḍito vigīta. Paṇḍita* is learned, whereas *vigīta* means contradictory or twisted, and so the expression refers to "twisted or contradictory learning," i.e., diplomacy.

[51] Here the eating of meat, even beef, is sanctioned.

[52] *Anumati* is the feminine personification of divine favor. See RV 10.167.3.

[53] Vishvavasu is the name of a Gandharva spirit who is the protector of virgins. See RV 10.85.22. After marriage he is asked to leave the bride, who is no longer to be under his care.

eyes, who is learned in three Vedas and who will have a long life, he should have his wife cook rice boiled only in water with clarified butter. Together they should eat this and it will make them capable to have such a child.

17. If he should desire a daughter who is learned[49] and who will have a long life, he should have his wife cook rice made with sesame and clarified butter. Together they should eat this and it will make them capable to have such a child.

18. If he should desire a learned son who is diplomatic[50] and who can speak at assemblies, who is learned in all the Vedas and who will have a long life, he should have his wife cook rice made with meat and, together with clarified butter, they should eat it. This will make them capable to have such a child. The meat can be from a calf or a bull.[51]

19. Then, during the early morning, let the man prepare a mixture of ghee and grains and make oblations, saying, "Hail to fire, hail to Anumati,[52] hail to the divine sun, the creator of truth." After making these oblations, the couple should eat what is left. After that the man must wash his hands and fill a pot with water and three times sprinkle his wife with that water and say:

"Arise, O Vishvavasu,[53] find another young girl.
This wife is now here with her husband."

Embracing his wife he says,

20. "I am he, you are she.
You are she, I am he.[54]
I am the Sama, you are the Rig.
I am the heaven, you are the earth.
Let us come together.
Let us give the seed.
Let us acquire a child who is a son."

21. He must then separate her thighs and think, "I separate heaven and earth." He places his member in her, joins his mouth with hers, strokes her three times and thinks:

"May Vishnu prepare your womb.
May Tvashta shape the forms.
May Prajapati pour in you.
May Dhatri place the seed.
O Sinivali, goddess of easy birth, place this embryo.
O Prithustuka, goddess with tufts of hair, place this embryo.
O Ashvanis, two gods with lotus garlands, place this embryo.

---

[54] Here the Sanskrit, *amo 'ham asmi sā tvam sā tvam asy amo 'ham,* is obscure. I have glossed *amah* as "he." Some commentators take *amah* as *prāna* and *sā* as speech, and so the line is often rendered as "I am breath, you are speech; you are speech, I am breath."
[55] The Vedic calendar was primarily based on the moon and not the sun, and so a child took ten lunar months to be born.
[56] Literally, the Sanskrit only says *jāte*, "on the birth," but the implied meaning is "on the birth of a male child."

22. "Those fire sticks of gold by which the Ashvins churned a flame,
That I call as the embryo to be born in ten months.[55]
As fire is the embryo within the earth,
As the sky is made pregnant by the storm,
As the wind is the embryo of the directions,
So I place this fetus in you."

23. When his wife is about to deliver he should sprinkle her with water and say:

"As the blowing wind disturbs a lotus pond,
May this embryo stir and be born along with its caul.
This sheath, fashioned by Indra, which surrounds this embryo,
Expel it, O Indra, along with this child and its caul."

24. After the birth[56] the man should kindle a fire and mix milk and clarified butter in a metal bowl. He must then place the child on his lap and make oblations into the fire, saying:

"With this child in my home, may prosperity increase a thousandfold.
Let him never lose his wealth of livestock and offspring. *Svaha*
In my mind I offer my breaths to you. *Svaha*
Whatever I have overdone in the performance of this rite, or not done enough, may Agni, the wise, the beneficent, make that good for us. *Svaha"*

25. Drawing close to the child's right ear, he should whisper

three times, "Speech, speech, speech!" He must then mix milk, yogurt, and clarified butter, and feed the child with a golden spoon, without touching the child's mouth. He says to the child, "I give you the earth, I give you the sky, I give you the heavens, I give you it all."

26. After this he must name his son: "You are to be known as so-and-so."[57] This name becomes the child's secret name.

27. Afterwards he passes his son to the child's mother, and, as she offers the child a breast, the father recites:

"O Sarasvati, your breast is ever-flowing and refreshing.
It is the bestower of wealth, treasures and gifts.
This breast by which you nourish whomever you choose on this earth, give that to this child for his nourishment."

28. To the child's mother he says:

---

[57] This is a rudimentary form of the name-giving ceremony, *nāma karaṇa.*

[58] It is not clear who Ila is. Some commentators identify her with Arundhatī, the wife of Vashishtha. Another reading suggests Ida the goddess of satisfaction mentioned in the RV.

[59] There are other teacher/student lineage lists at BU 2.6 and 4.6. These kinds of lists are called *paraṃparas* and they are meant to show the authenticity of the teachings. Such lists always begin with God or, in this case, *brahma.*

[60] This list is unusual because it is a list descending from mothers. The previous lists (BU 2.6 and 4.6) are lists descending from male teachers.

"You are Ila, born in the family of Mitra and Varuna.[58]
O heroic lady, you have given birth to a hero.
You have made me the father of a hero.
May you continue to be the mother of heroes."

They say of such a son, indeed, he has surpassed his father. Indeed, he has surpassed his grandfather! A son who is born in the family of *brāhmanas* who have this knowledge has reached the very limits of splendor, fame and spiritual power.

Here ends the fourth *Brāhmaṇa* of the sixth *Adhyāya*

Fifth *Brāhmaṇa*

The Lineage of Teachers and Students in the
Vājaseneyi School[59]

1. Now the lineage:
The son of Pautimāṣī[60] received these teachings from the son of Kātyāyanī,
the son of Kātyāyanī from the son of Gautamī,
the son of Gautamī from the son of Bhāradvājī,
the son of Bhāradvājī from the son of Pārāśarī,
the son of Pārāśarī from the son of Aupasvastī,
the son of Aupasvastī from the son of Kātyāyanī,
the son of Kātyāyanī from the son of Kauśikī,
the son of Kauśikī from the son of Ālambī and the son of Vaiyāghrapadī,
the son of Vaiyāghrapadī from the son of Kāṇvī and the son of Kāpī,

the son of Kāpī (2) from the son of Ātreyī,
the son of Ātreyī from the son of Gautamī,
the son of Gautamī from the son of Bhāradvājī,
the son of Bhāradvājī from the son of Pārāśarī,
the son of Pārāśarī from the son of Vātsī,
the son of Vātsī from the son of Pārāśarī,
the son of Pārāśarī from the son of Vārkāruṇī,
the son of Vārkāruṇī from the son of Vārkāruṇī,
the son of Vārkāruṇī from the son Ārtabhāgī,
the son of Ārtabhāgī from the son of Śauṅgī,
the son of Śauṅgī from the son of Sāṅkrtī,
the son of Sāṅkrtī from the son of Ālambāyanī,
the son of Ālambāyanī from the son of Ālambī,
the son of Ālambī from the son of Jāyantī,
the son of Jāyantī from the son of Māṇḍūkāyanī,
the son of Māṇḍūkāyanī from the son of Māṇḍūkī,
the son of Māṇḍūkī from the son of Śāṇḍilī,
the son of Śāṇḍilī from the son of Rāthītarī,
the son of Rāthītarī from the son of Bhālukī,
the son of Bhālukī from the two sons of Krauñcikī,
the two sons of Krauñcikī from the son of Vaidabhṛtī,
the son of Vaidabhṛtī from the son of Kārśakeyī,
the son of Kārśakeyī from the son of Prācīnayogī,
the son of Prācīnayogī from the son of Sāñjīvī,
the son of Sāñjīvī from Āsurivāsin, the son of Prāśnī,
the son of Prāśnī from Āsurāyaṇa,
Āsurāyaṇa from Āsuri,

[61] This succession reflects the tradition from the Shukla Yajur Veda as opposed to the Krishna Yajur Veda.

Āsuri (3) from Yajnavalkya,
Yajnavalkya from Uddālaka,
Uddālaka from Aruṇa,
Aruṇa from Upaveśi,
Upaveśi from Kuśri,
Kuśri from Vājaśravas,
Vājaśravas from Jihvāvat Bādhyoga,
Jihvāvat Bādhyoga from Asita Vārṣagaṇa,
Asita Vārṣagaṇa from Harita Kaśyapa,
Harita Kaśyapa from Śilpa Kaśyapa,
Śilpa Kaśyapa from Kaśyapa Naidhruvi,
Kaśyapa Naidhruvi from Vāc,
Vāc from Ambhiṇī,
Ambhiṇī from Āditya, the Sun.

These white sacrificial formulas (*yajur*)[61] which come from the sun (*āditya*) are declared by Yajnavalkya of the Vajasaneyi school.

4. Up to the son of Sāñjivī it is the same.
The son of Sāñjivī from Māṇḍūkāyani,
Māṇḍūkāyani from Māṇḍavya,
Māṇḍavya from Kautsa,
Kautsa from Māhitthi,
Māhitthi from Vāmakakṣāyaṇa,
Vāmakakṣāyaṇa from Śāṇḍilya,
Śāṇḍilya from Vātsya,
Vātsya from Kuśri,
Kuśri from Yajñavacas Rājastambāyana,
Yajñavacas Rājastambāyana from Tura Kāvaṣeya,

Tura Kāvaṣeya from Prajapati,
Prajapati from *brahma*.
Brahma is Self-existent. Adoration to *brahma*!

Here ends the fifth *Brāhmaṇa* of the sixth *Adhyāya*
Here ends the sixth *Adhyāya*
Here ends the *Brihad Aranyaka Upanishad*

Sanskrit Glossary

ācārya–traditional teacher or theologian of Hindu doctrine, head of *sampradāya* or school of religious thought.

adharma–the opposite of *dharma*. The term is often used in the sense of unrighteousness, impiety or non-performance of duty.

adhibhūta–the manifestation of *brahma* as the perishable nature of matter.

adhidaiva–the manifestation of *brahma* as the Universal Person or *puruṣa* who is the foundation of the gods.

adhiyajña–the principle of divinity that dwells within all things and is the recipient of all sacrifice.

adhyātmā–the manifestation of *brahma* as the individual soul.

advaita–non dualism, the name given to the theological position of the Shankara school of thought.

agni–fire or the fire deity.

ahimsā–nonviolence.

akṣara–something that is imperishable, the soul, God.

āryan–one of noble birth, one faithful to the religion of the Vedas.

artha–wealth, not to be understood solely as material assets, but all kinds of wealth including non-tangibles such as knowledge, friendship and love. *Artha* is one of the four *puruṣārthas* or "goals of life," the others being *dharma*, *kāma* and *mokṣa*.

āśrama–one of the four stages of life: *brahmacarya* (studentship), *gārhasthya* (householder), *vānaprastha* (retired), and *sannyāsa* (renounced); a hermitage.

asat–opposite of *sat,* non-being, impermanent, false, evil, unreal, sometimes used to refer to matter or to the body.

asura–an ungodly one, a demon, one who does not follow the path of the Vedas.

ātman–has many meanings in Sanskrit that include: soul, breath, the Self, one's self (as a reflexive pronoun), mind, body, the Supreme Soul, etc.

avatāra–literally, one who descends, an incarnation of God who descends into this physical world, an incarnation of Viṣṇu.

avidyā–non knowledge, ignorance, nescience.

bhagavān–literally, one possessed of *bhaga. Bhaga* means fame, glory, strength, power, etc. The word is used as an epithet applied to God, gods, or any holy or venerable personality.

bhakta–a devotee, one who follows the path of devotion.

bhakti–love, devotion. One of the most common forms of *yoga.*

bhakti-yoga–the spiritual path of connecting one's self to God through devotion.

brahmā–the four headed creator god born of the lotus.

brahmacārī–a religious student in the first stage of life.

brahmacarya–the first stage of life, studentship, celibacy.

brahman–derived from the Sanskrit root *bṛmh* meaning to grow, to expand, to bellow, to roar. The word *brahman* refers to the Supreme Principle regarded as impersonal and divested of all qualities. *Brahman* is the essence from which all created beings are produced and into which they are absorbed. This word is neuter and not to be confused with the masculine word Brahmā, the creator god. *Brahman* is sometimes used to denote the syllable *om* or the *Vedas* in general.

brāhmaṇa–a member of the traditional priestly class. The *brāhmaṇa* was the first of the four *varṇas* in the social system called *varṇāśrama- dharma.* Literally, the word means "in relation to brahman." A *brāhmaṇa* is one who follows the ways of *brahman*. Traditionally a *brāhmaṇa*, often written as brahmin, filled the role of priest, teacher and thinker.

candra–the moon or the moon deity.

deva–derived from the Sanskrit root *div* meaning to shine or become bright. A *deva* is therefore a "shining one." The word is used to refer to God, a god or any exalted personality. The female version is *devī*.

devanāgarī–name of the writing script in which Sanskrit and Hindi are usually written.

dharma–derived from the Sanskrit root *dhṛ* meaning to hold up, to carry, to bear, to sustain. The word *dharma* refers to that which upholds or sustains the universe. Human society, for example, is sustained and upheld by the *dharma* performed by its members. Parents protecting and maintaining children, children being obedient to parents, the king protecting the citizens are acts of *dharma* that uphold and sustain society. In this context *dharma* has the meaning of duty. *Dharma* also employs the meaning of law, religion, virtue, and ethics. These things uphold and sustain the proper functioning of human society. In philosophy *dharma* refers to the defining quality of an object. For instance, liquidity is one of the essential *dharmas* of water; coldness is a *dharma* of ice. In this case we can think that the existence of an object is sustained or defined by its essential attributes, *dharmas*.

duḥkha–suffering or unhappiness.

dvaita–dualism, the name given to the theological position of the Mādhva school of thought.

dvāpara-yuga–the third time period (*yuga*) said to last 864,000 years (two times 432,000)

gaṅgā–the river Ganges.

gārhasthya–the third order (*āśrama*) of life, domestic affairs.

gāyatrī–a meter used throughout the Vedas comprised of three lines of eight measures totaling twenty-four measures. A sacred chant.

guṇa–quality, positive attributes or virtues. In the context of Bhagavad Gita and *Sāṅkhya* philosophy there are three *guṇas* of matter. Sometimes *guṇa* is translated as phase or mode. Therefore the three *guṇas* or phases of matter are: *sattva-guṇa, rajo-guṇa* and *tamo- guṇa*. The word *guṇa* also means a rope or thread and it is sometimes said that beings are "roped" or "tied" into matter by the three *guṇas* of material nature.

gṛhastha–one situated in the second order of life (*āśrama*), a householder.

guru–a teacher. Literally, the word means heavy and so refers to one "heavy" with knowledge, commonly used to refer to a spiritual teacher.

haṭha-yoga–a path of physical discipline meant to control the senses.

Īśā–literally, lord, master, or controller. *Īśā* is one of the words used for God as the supreme controller. The word is also used to refer to any being or personality who is in control.

Īśvara–see Īśā.

japa–chanting.

jīva–the soul, a living being.

jñāna–derived from the Sanskrit root *jñā*, to know, to learn, to experience. In the context of Bhagavad Gita and the Upanishads, *jñāna* is generally used in the sense of spiritual knowledge or awareness.

jñāna-yoga–the spiritual path of connecting one's self to God through knowledge.

jñānī–literally, "one possessed of knowledge," a scholar.

kāma–wish, desire, love. Often used in the sense of sexual desire or love, but not necessarily. *Kāma* is one of the four *puruṣārthas* or "goals of life," the others being *dharma, artha* and *mokṣa.*

kāla–time.

kali-yuga–one of the four ages, said to last 432,000 years, the age characterized by fighting and diminished spiritual abilities.

kalpa–sacred law, a period of time, a twelve hour period (a day) of Brahmā said to last one thousand *mahā-yuga* cycles.

karma–derived from the Sanskrit root *kṛ* meaning to do, to make. The work *karma* means action, work, and deed. Only secondarily does *karma* refer to the result of past deeds, which are more properly known as the *phalam* or fruit of action.

karma-yoga–the spiritual path of connecting one's self to God through action or work.

kṣatriya–a member of the traditional military or warrior class. A king, a prince. The *kṣatriya* was the second *varṇa* in the system of *varṇāśrama-dharma.*

kṣara–something that is perishable, the body, the world.

kṣetra–a field, the body, the world.

kṣetra-jña–the knower of the field, the soul, God.

līlā–divine pastime, play of God.

mahā-yuga–a period of time comprised of one cycle of the four *yugas: satya, tretā, dvāpara* and *kali*, a total of 4,320,000 years.

mantra–a Vedic hymn or sacred prayer.

māyā–a trick, illusion.

mokṣa–liberation or freedom of rebirth. *Mokṣa* is one of the four *puruśārthas* or "goals of life," the others being *dharma*, *artha* and *kāma*.

mukti–see *mokṣa*.

muni–a sage, a silent one.

nirguṇa–without attributes, refers to God conceived to be impersonal.

nirvāṇa–blown out or extinguished as in the case of a lamp. *Nirvāṇa* is generally used to refer to a material life that has been extinguished, one who has achieved freedom from re-birth. The term *nirvāṇa* is commonly used in Buddhism as the final stage a practitioner strives for. The word does not mean heaven.

om–a sacred syllable, the sound of *brahman*, a sound vibrated at the beginning and end of Vedic recitation, the Vedas.

pāpa–literally, *pāpa* is what brings one down. Sometimes translated as sin or evil.

paramātman–the supreme soul, the supersoul, the lord of the heart, an aspect of God that pervades all things.

paramparā–one following the other, the chain of teachers and disciples.

pitṛ–a father, a forefather, an ancestor, a class of celestial beings, the manes.

prakṛti–material nature. In *sāṅkhya* philosophy *prakṛti* is comprised of eight elements: earth, water, fire, air, space, mind, intellect and ego. It is characterized by the three *guṇas*: *sattva*, *rajas* and *tamas*. *Prakṛti* is female. *Puruṣa* is male.

prāṇa–breath, life force, the senses.

prasāda–favor, mercy, blessing, God's blessings, any item that has been offered to God during worship, especially food.

puṇya–the opposite to *pāpa*. *Puṇya* is what elevates; it is virtue or moral merit. *Pāpa* and *puṇya* go together as negative and positive "credits." One reaps the reward of these negative or positive credits in life. The more *puṇya* one cultivates the higher one rises in life, whereas *pāpa* will cause one to find a lower position. *Puṇya* leads to happiness, *pāpa* leads to suffering.

puruṣa–man, male. In *sāṅkhya* philosophy *puruṣa* denotes the Supreme Male Principle in the universe. Its counterpart is *prakṛti*.

puruṣottama–comprised of two words: *puruṣa* + *uttama* literally meaning "highest man." *Puruṣottama* means God.

rajas–the second of the three *guṇas* of matter. Sometimes translated as passion, the phase of *rajas* is characterized by action, passion, creation, etc.

ṛta–what is proper, right, true, divine law.

ṛtu–season, a period of time, menstruation period.

ṛṣi–an inspired poet or sage, a class of beings distinct from men and gods who were the "seers" of the Vedas.

saṅkhya–calculating, enumeration, analysis, categorization. Modern science can be said to be a form of *saṅkhya* because it attempts to analyze and categorize matter into its constituent elements. *Sāṅkhya* (first *a* long) refers to an ancient system of philosophy attributed to the sage Kapila. This philosophy is so called because it enumerates or analyses reality into a set number of basic elements, similar to modern science.

saguṇa–literally, "with attributes," God conceived as possessing humanlike qualities.

śaiva–a follower of Śiva.

śākta–a follower of Durgā (*śakti*).

śakti–power, energy conceived as female in nature.

samādhi–meditative trance, absorption in the divine.

sannyāsī–one situated in the final stage (*āśrama*) of life, a mendicant.

sannyāsa–the fourth or final stage (*āśrama*) of life, characterized by full renunciation.

śāstra–an order, command, rule, scriptural injunction, sacred writings, science, any department of knowledge.

sat–being, good, virtuous, chaste, the third word of the famous three words: *oṃ tat sat,* refers to what is truly real, eternal and permanent, used to mean God or the soul.

sattva–the first of the three *guṇas* of matter. Sometimes translated as goodness, the phase of *sattva* is characterized by lightness, peace, cleanliness, knowledge, etc.

satyam–truth. The word *satyam* is formed from *sat* with the added abstract suffix *ya*. *Sat* refers to what is true and real. The abstract suffix *ya* means "ness." Thus *satyam* literally means trueness or realness.

satya-yuga–the first of the four *yugas*, said to comprise 1,728,000 years, characterized by virtue, wisdom and spirituality.

śloka–a hymn or verse of praise, a stanza or verse in general, a stanza in *anuṣṭubh* metre (the most common metre used in Sanskrit consisting for 4 lines of 8 syllables), fame.

smṛti–literally, "what is heard," the division of the Vedas written by human beings (*pauruṣeya*), comprised of the later tradition that includes the Mahabharata, Ramayana, Puranas etc.

śruti–literally, "what is heard," the division of the Vedas not written by human beings (*apauruṣeya*), said to be "heard" by the *ṛṣis*, comprised of the four Vedas including the Upanishads.

śūdra–a member of the traditional working class. The śūdra was the fourth *varṇa* in the system of *varṇāśrama-dharma.*

sukha–happiness, pleasure.

sura–a godly one, a god, one who follows the path of the Vedas.

svāmī–controller, a *yogī*, one in the renounced stage of life, a *guru.*

tamas–the third of the three *guṇas* of matter. Sometimes translated as darkness, the phase of *tamas* is characterized by darkness, ignorance, slowness, destruction, heaviness, disease, etc.

tapas–heat, voluntary acceptance of trouble for a spiritual goal, austerity, penance.

tapasya–see *tapas.*

tretā-yuga–the second of the four *yugas*, said to last 1,296,000 years.

tyāga–abandonment, renunciation, the performance of actions without attachment to the results of action.

vaikuṇṭha–literally, "without anxiety," the realm or heaven of Viṣṇu.

vairāgya–renounciation, detachment from the world.

vaiṣṇava–a follower of Viṣṇu.

vaiśya–a member of the traditional mercantile or business community. The *vaiśya* was the third *varṇa* in the system of *varṇāśrama-dharma.*

vānaprastha–the third order (*āśrama*) of life, the retired stage. Literally, "one who remains in the forest."

varṇāśrama–the traditional social system of four *varṇas* and four *aśramas*. The word *varṇa* literally means, "color" and it refers to four basic natures of mankind: *brāhmaṇa*, *kṣatriya*, *vaiśya* and *śūdra*. The *āśramas* are the four stages of an individual's life: *brahmacarya* (student), *gṛhastha* (householder), *va-*

naprastha (retired) and *sannyāsa* (renounced).

veda(s)–knowledge, the sacred knowledge of the āryans, the Hindu scriptures, the Rig, Yajur, Sama, Atharva, Mahabharata, Ramayana, Puranas, Vedanta-sutra, etc.

vidyā–knowledge, the goddess Sarasvatī.

vijñāna–derived from the prefix *vi* added to the noun *jñāna*. The prefix *vi* added to a noun tends to diminish or invert the meaning of a word. If *jñāna* is spiritual knowledge, *vijñāna* is practical or profane knowledge. Sometimes *vijñāna* and *jñāna* are used together in the sense of knowledge and wisdom.

viśiṣṭādvaita–often translated as "oneness of the organic unity" or "differentiated monism," the theology taught by the Śrī Vaiṣṇavism associated with Rāmānuja.

viśva-rūpa–God's cosmic form, the universal form, the vision seen by Arjuna in Bhagavad Gita Chapter Eleven.

yajña–sacrifice, the worship of God performed with fire.

yoga–derived from the Sanskrit root *yuj*, to join, to unite, to attach. The English word yoke is cognate with the Sanskrit word *yoga*. We can think of *yoga* as the joining of the *ātman* with the *paramātman*, the soul with God. There are numerous means of joining with God: through action, *karma-yoga*; through knowledge, *jñāna-yoga*; through devotion, *bhakti-yoga*; through meditation, *dhyāna-yoga*, etc. *Yoga* has many other meanings. For example, in astronomy and astrology it refers to a conjunction (union) of planets.

yogī–literally, one possessed of *yoga*. A *yogī* is a practitioner of *yoga*.

yuga–a period of time said to comprise 432,000 years, one of the four ages that rotate like calendar seasons.

Index

A

action, 6, 40
  good and evil, 77, 137
  memories of past, 136
agni-hotra, see fire sacrifice
ancestors (forefathers),
  are mind, 34
  ātmā, 141n
  libations to, 29
  path to, 177, 182
  world of (*Pitṛ-loka),* 36, 71n, 72, 132
Aryans, 3
asat (unreal),
  asuras embrace, 157n;
  lead from unreal to real, 20
  meaning changed, xxx-xxxi
  never harmed by, 158
  non-being, 5n
  this world, 39n, 47n, 84n
astral body, 49n, 63n, 77n, 121n, 125n, 127n, 133n, 181n
asuras, see demons
aśva-medha, see horse sacrifice
ātmā, (self, soul)
  as the Real, 28, 40, 48
  brings joy, 57
  knower of, 140-144
  leaves the body, 136
  love of, 145-146
  meaning contextual, 5n, 55n
  mind is, 29
  I am, 20
  indestructible, 122, 148
  immortal, 60-62,
  imperishable, 129-131
  the immortal force, 87-91
  soul, self, 97n
  trail to all things, 24
  within all, 79-82
austerity, 8, 30, 142
avidyā, (ignorance) 135, **139-140**, 143n
Ayasya Angirasa, 13-16, 18

B

boon, 20, 178-179
brahma,
  ātmā within all, 79-80
  felt alone, xxviii
  food is, 162
  honey teachings, 60-65
  knower of, 141-144
  hṛdaya, the heart, 156
  is lightening, 159
  manifest, 25-28
  meaning contextual, 17n,
  obtained by worship of, 42-46
  sum total of learning, 36

that, 152, 155
two forms of, 51-54
ultimate force, xxiii
what is *brahma*, 112-119
world of (*brahma-lokah*), 133
brahman, 17n
Brahmanaspati, Lord of speech, 18
Brahmā (creator god), viii, 17n, 23n, 67n, 83n, 133n
brāhmana (priestly caste), 25-26, 28, 45n, 81-81, 145, 179, 194
breath, 11, 13-19, 33-34, 37-40, 49, 73-75, 79-80, 86, 107
Brihaspati, 18

C

Campbell, Joseph, xxix
caterpillar metaphor, 136
charity, 142, 154-155, 182
compassion, 2, 164-155
consciousness, 1, 46-48, 127n, 135-136, 142, 147n
creation,
agni-hotra, xxvii
cremation, 265
myth, 5-9, 20-30
of evil, 10-20
progenitors, 83n, 156-158
reason for, xxviii

D

da da da (restraint, charity, compassion), 153-155
Darwin, Charles, xxi
death,
all-devouring, 8
avoid repeated, 79,
after death, 59, 109-110, 148, 176-184
is the unreal, 20
time of, 157n, 158, 160
transcend, 124
overcome, 32, 69, 76, 161n
Yama, god of, 104
Death (the divinity), 5-10
demons (*asuras),* 4, 9-14, 141, 153-155
desire, 28-29, 33, 34, 75-76, 82, 128-129, 132-133, 136-144,
destiny, 140
Deva-loka (world of the gods), 71-72
dharma, 27-28, 62
directions, 16, 61, 88, 117, 122, 198
disease, 134, 161
dreams, 124-134
duality, 59, 131n, 135n, 148, 157n
Dur, 13-15

dying,
process of, 135-144
prayer of, 170

E

evil (*pāpa),*
actions, 137, 142-143,
bad deeds, 77
brahma cuts all, 159
creation of, 10-15
cruel humans, 153n
death is, 40
food possessed of, 31
never goes to the gods, 37
good and, 124-129, 134
good triumphs over, 157n
eye, path to the soul, 69-70

F

falsehoods, 11
fasting, 142, 183n
father (*pitā*), 29n,
is mind, 34
mixed breed, 129
of a hero, 200
son delivers, 36-37
son resembles, 106
father heaven, 177
fear, 21, 33, 115, 128, 148
fearless, 122, 129, 142, 144
fire sacrifice (*agni-hotra),*
food offered, 31
for greatness, 184-190
for power, xxviii-xxix
hymns (High Chant), 9n
leads to liberation, 69-72
libations, 28-29
main priests, 68-74
metaphor for life, 179-182
shaped Vedic worldview,
xxvi-xxviii
Upanishads emphasize, xxiv
woman as, 179n, 181
food,
accumulated tradition, xx
digest, 160
foundation of life, 16, 19
life force, 162
seven kinds of, 30-33
world is food for death, 76
forefathers, see ancestors
form, 6, 24, 26, 40-41, 52-54,
64, 75, 104, 126, 147
from the unreal lead me to real
(*asato mā sad gamaya*), 20
fullness, 152

G

Gandharva, 4, 78, 83, 85-86,
132, 174n, 195n
gāyatrī, 73n, 163-168, 185n
gods (*devas*),
addressed as *bhagavān,* 55n
compete with demons, 10-20
evil never goes to, 37

fire sacrifice, xxx, 9, 28
go to, 113-120
goldsmith metaphor, 199
number of, 95-100, 108
offer to, 30-36
path to, 177
restraint (*dāmyata*), 153-154
so man is to, 26
steed carries, 4
superior, 23
world of (*Deva-loka)*, 71-72, 84, 132
gotra (paternal lineage), 177n
greatness, 97n, 143, 184-190

H

havan, see fire sacrifice
hearing, 12, 24, 57, 116-117, 141, 172-174
heart, 47n, 48, 62, 100-107, 119, 120, 124, 135-138, 147, 156
High Chant, xxvii, 9-18, 187
homa, see fire sacrifice
Honey Teachings, 60-65
horse head, 63-64
Horse Sacrifice (*aśva-medha),* xxvii, **3-4**, 6n, 8-10
performers of, 78
sacrificial animal, 29, 99
humans, 153-154
humanity, 62
husband, 22, 51n, 56, 145, 196

I

ignorance, 136, 139n, 140
see *avidyā*,
immortal, 41, 52-54, 60-62, 87-91, 100, 126
immortality, 20, 56, 141, 144-145
imperishable, 50, 94-95, 130-131, 174
Indra, 23n, 26, 34, 44, 50, 51n, 96n, 97, 78, 84, 98, 121

J

joy, 21, 37, 55-57, 118, 125, 132-133

K

kindness, 153n
King Soma, 18, 43, 46, 180, 182
knowledge (*vidyā*), xv, 25, 28-30, 36, 139-143, 144, 168-170, 180, 195n
ksạtriya, 28, 57, 129n, 145, 179

L

language, xxviii, 8, 163n
liberation, 69-70, 137n

life after death, 176-184
light of man, 122-134
lightning, 4, 43, 54, 61, 98-99, 159, 180, 182
law, 27n, 39

M

man, xxv, 21, 26, 36-38, 109-110, 180
malice, 168
māyā, xxxi, 157n
meditation, 2, 129
mind, 8-9, 12-13, 16, 29, 32-37, 75-77, 90, 100-103, 118, 137, 147, 173-175
moon, 16, 31, 39, 94, 98, 123-124, 161, 180-184
mortal life, 161-162
Mother earth, 177

N

neti, neti, (not this, not this) 53-54, 93-94, 107-108, 121-122, 141-142

O

oblations, 71-72, 113, 147
outcastes, 141n, 183n

P

pāpa, 36
paramātmā, 159n
path of darkness 182
path of light 182
plurality, 5n, 141n
Prajapati, 10, 23n, 29n, 31, 35, 42n, 98, 103, 153, 156
Prajapatis, The, 84, 103,
prāṇa (life force), 33, 73n, 75n, 79n, 97n, 107n, 124, 135, 161n, 166
pratiloma, 45n
procreation, 173-175, 183n, 190-200
puruṣa, 19n
putra, 36

R

rakṣasas, 141n
rasa, 7
real, see *sat*
religion of affirmation, xxix-xxxi
restraint, 187-188
rite of transference, 36-37
Rudra, 26, 50
Rudras, 27, 98

S

sat (real), xxx-xxxi, 5n, 39n, 41n, 47n, 51n, 54, 147n, 155n, 157n, 158
satya (truth), 155n, 158
semen, 6n, 8, 22, 60, 77, 91, 103, 106, 109, 173-175, 181, 190-194
senses, 38, 74-77, 98, 166
Seven Sages, 50
sexual rituals, see procreation
Shiva, 17n, 27n
sight, 11, 24, 40, 104, 115-116, 172-174
Smith, Wilford Cantwell, xx
sleep, 46-48, 124-129,
snake skin metaphor, 138
soma, 21n, 43, 71n, 131n, 190-191
son (*putra*), 35n, 36-37, 56-57, 82, 106, 118, 142, 145, 195-200
soul, xxiv-xxvi, xxviii-xxxi, 5n, 35n, 37, 39n, 49n, 53n, 55n, 108, 135n,
caterpillar metaphor, 136
southern path, 181n
space, 88, 94-95, 98-99, 182
speech, 4, 8, 10-11, 24, 32-34, 38, 52, 69, 113, 160, 163n, 198-199
śūdra, 28, 129n, 173-175,
sun, 4, 15, 26, 34, 38-39, 83n, 88, 98, 123-124, 158, 160-161, 180-184
sun's chariot, 78

T

Theory of evolution, xxi
Three Worlds, The, 18, 33, 36, 87n, 99
theological interpretation, 17
thought, 24, 141, 173-174
truth (*satya*), xxx-xxxi, 28, 62, 101, 106, 116, 155n, 166, 170

U

universal soul, xxvi
universe, body of God, 3n, 4, 157n
unreal, see *asat*

V

vaiśya, 28
varṇas, 28, 81n, 141n
Varuna, 26, 105, 200
Vasus, 27, 42n, 97n, 98
vidyā, (knowledge) 140, 143n
Vishnu, xxiii, 17n, 23n, 197

W

warp and woof, 81n, 82-84, 92-95
wealth, 18-19, 29, 35, 50, 56-57, 82, 98, 112n, 132, 142-145
wife, 22, 29, 56, 85, 118, 145, 190-200
wisdom, 113, 153
woman,
  approached for intimacy, 192-195
  as sacrificial fire, 179n, 181
  creation of, 21-22,
  learn sacred knowledge, 195
  Prajapati created, 190-191
worlds,
  of the gods (*Deva-loka*), 72, 84, 132
  of the ancestors (*Pitṛ-loka*), 72, 132
  of men (*Manuṣya-loka*), 72

Y

Yama, god of death, 26, 104

Z

zenith, 107, 122

Twelve Essential Upanishads

Three Volume Series

English translation with annotations

Shukavak N. Dasa

Volume I
Brihad Aranyaka Upanishad:
The Forest Teachings

Volume II
Chandogya Upanishad:
Teachings from the High Chant

Volume III
Taitiriya, Aitareya, Kaushitaki,
Kena, Katha, Isha, Shvetashvatara,
Mundaka, Prashna, and Mandukya
Upanishads

ISBN 978-1-889756-00-4

Ganga Flows West

A Hindu Primer

An easy to read and simple explanation of the most important points of Hinduism.

by Shukavak N. Dasa

"I've seen that ritual a hundred times, this however, is the first time I understood its meaning"

Hindu Encounter with Modernity

Kedarnath Datta Bhaktivinoda, Vaiṣṇava Theologian

Nineteen century India was a time of great religious and cultural change as European religions and philosophies spread throughout the Indian subcontinent. Through the eyes of one Hindu religious reformer, Kedarnath Datta Bhaktivinoda, *Hindu Encounter with Modernity* is a study of how Hinduism evolved and adapted to Western culture and ideas.

Bhaktivinoda's life straddled contemporary British society and ancestral Hindu culture. One was a modern, analytical world which demanded rational thought. The other was a traditional world of Hindu faith and piety, which seemingly allowed little room for critical analysis. Could he play a meaningful role in modern society and at the same time maintain integrity as a Hindu? ISBN 978-1-889756-30-1

www.ingramcontent.com/pod-product-compliance
Lightning Source LLC
Chambersburg PA
CBHW041305110526
44590CB00028B/4249
* 9 7 8 1 8 8 9 7 5 6 0 0 4 *